PENGUIN M...

Guest Edi...

Kenward Elmslie was born in...
Colorado Springs, and gradua...
include *The Baby Book* (1965), *The 1967 Gamebook Calendar*, *The Champ* (1968) (all in collaboration with Joe Brainard); *Album* (1969); *Circus Nerves* (1971); *Motor Disturbance*, which won the 1971 Frank O'Hara Award for Poetry, and a novel, *The Orchid Stories* (1973). His theatre works include four opera librettos: *The Sweet Bye and Bye*, *Lizzie Borden*, *Miss Julie* and *The Seagull*; *The Grass Harp*, a musical play based on the novel by Truman Capote; and *City Junket*, a play. He has won a Ford Foundation Grant and a National Council on the Arts Award. He lives in New York and in Calais, Vermont.

Kenneth Koch was born in Cincinnati, Ohio, in 1925 and educated at Harvard and Columbia. He has been teaching English and Comparative Literature at Columbia since 1959. His books include *Ko, or A Season on Earth* (1959), *Permanently* (1961), *Thank You and Other Poems* (1962), *Bertha and Other Plays* (1966), *The Pleasures of Peace* (1969), and *Wishes, Lies and Dreams* (1970). He has had a number of plays produced and is at present working on a novel, *The Red Robins*.

James Schuyler was born in Chicago in 1923 but grew up in Washington, D.C., and western New York State. He lived for several years in Italy and was formerly on the staff of the Museum of Modern Art and of *Art News Magazine*, to which he still contributes. His books of poetry include *Salute*, *May 24th Or So*, *Freely Espousing*, and *The Crystal Lithium*. He has published two novels, *Alfred and Guinevere* and *A Nest of Ninnies* (with John Ashbery). He has received a number of awards, including a creative writing grant in 1972 from the National Endowment for the Arts. He lives in Long Island and in New York City.

Penguin Modern Poets

— 24 —

KENWARD ELMSLIE

KENNETH KOCH

JAMES SCHUYLER

—

Guest Editor:
JOHN ASHBERY

Penguin Books

Penguin Books Ltd, Harmondsworth, Middlesex, England
Penguin Books Inc., 7110 Ambassador Road, Baltimore, Maryland 21207, U.S.A.
Penguin Books Australia Ltd, Ringwood, Victoria, Australia
Penguin Books Canada Ltd, 41 Steelcase Road West, Markham, Ontario, Canada

—

This selection first published 1974

—

—

Made and printed in Great Britain
by Richard Clay (The Chaucer Press) Ltd,
Bungay, Suffolk
Set in Monotype Garamond

Contents

Acknowledgements   9

KENWARD ELMSLIE

Circus Nerves and Worries   13
Ancestor Worship   14
Fringe People   16
Communique for Orpheus   17
Nov 25   21
The Champ (Part I)   23
Revolutionary Letter   28
Paper Suns   30
White Attic   32
Japanese City   33
Shirley Temple Surrounded by Lions   36
Feathered Dancers   38
Night Soil   41
Jan 24   43
Motor Disturbance   46
Chinese Creep   49
Girl Machine   51
Ground Hog Day Pensée   58
Hand   59
Eventual Bruises   60
Air   61
Tropicalism   62

KENNETH KOCH

Sleeping with Women   75
In Love with You   82
The Circus   84
The Artist   90

CONTENTS

Fresh Air   100
Permanently   109
You Were Wearing   110
Thank You   111
Lunch   114
Taking a Walk with You   120
The Departure from Hydra   125
The Pleasures of Peace   132
Alive for an Instant   147

JAMES SCHUYLER

Empathy and New Year   151
In January   155
A Sun Cab   156
Scarlet Tanager   158
Blue   160
Light Blue Above   161
After Joe Was at the Island   163
The Edge in the Morning   164
'Used Handkerchiefs 5¢'   166
Light from Canada   167
Closed Gentian Distances   168
Evening Wind   169
A Penis Moon   171
Verge   172
Running Footsteps   174
The Dog Wants His Dinner   176
The Crystal Lithium   178
Janis Joplin's Dead: Long Live Pearl   184
Eyes   186
The Night   188
Like Lorraine Ellison   190
Letter Poem #2   191

CONTENTS

Letter Poem #3   192
Fabergé   193
A White City   194
December   195
Ilford Rose Book   197
A Man in Blue   198
April and Its Forsythia   200
Sorting, wrapping, packing, stuffing   202
Crocus Night   205
Milk   206
Poem   208
3/23/66   209
Now and Then   210

Acknowledgements

The extract from *The Champ*, by Kenward Elmslie, is copyright
© 1968 by Kenward Elmslie and published by Black Sparrow
Press, Los Angeles; 'Revolutionary Letter', 'Paper Suns' and
'White Attic' are taken from *Album*, 1969, published by Kulchur
Press, New York; the following poems from *Circus Nerves*,
copyright © 1971 by Kenward Elmslie and published by Black
Sparrow Press, Los Angeles: 'Circus Nerves and Worries',
'Ancestor Worship', 'Fringe People', 'Communique for Or-
pheus', 'Nov 25'; the following poems from *Motor Disturbance*,
copyright © 1971, published by Columbia University Press,
New York: 'Japanese City', 'Shirley Temple Surrounded by
Lions', 'Feathered Dancers', 'Night Soil', 'Jan 24', 'Motor
Disturbance', 'Chinese Creep', 'Girl Machine'. 'Ground Hog
Day Pensée', and 'Eventual Bruises' first appeared in the maga-
zine *Adventures in Poetry*. 'Hand' first appeared in the magazine
Big Sky. 'Tropicalism' first appeared in the *Paris Review*. Grateful
acknowledgement is due to the author and the publishers for
permission to include these poems.

The poems of Kenneth Koch, with the exception of 'Sleeping
with Women' and 'The Pleasures of Peace' which come from
The Pleasures of Peace, copyright © Kenneth Koch, 1969, and
published by Grove Press, New York, and 'Alive for an Instant',
copyright © 1972 by Kenneth Koch and first published in the
New York Review of Books, are all taken from *Thank You and Other
Poems*, copyright © Kenneth Koch, 1962, and published by
Grove Press, New York. Grateful acknowledgement is due to
the author and the publishers for permission to include these
poems.

The following poems by James Schuyler are taken from *Freely
Espousing*, copyright © 1953, 1954, 1960, 1964, 1965, 1968, 1969
by James Schuyler and published by Doubleday, New York:
'Fabergé', 'A White City', 'December', 'Ilford Rose Book',
'A Man in Blue', 'April and Its Forsythia', 'Sorting, wrapping,

ACKNOWLEDGEMENTS

packing, stuffing', 'Crocus Night', 'Milk', 'Poem', '3/23/66', 'Now and Then'. The following poems are taken from *The Crystal Lithium*, copyright © 1972 by James Schuyler and published by Random House, New York: 'Empathy and New Year', 'In January', 'A Sun Cab', 'Scarlet Tanager', 'Blue', 'Light Blue Above', 'After Joe Was at the Island', 'The Edge in the Morning', 'Used Handkerchiefs 5¢', 'Light from Canada', 'Closed Gentian Distances', 'Evening Wind', 'A Penis Moon', 'Verge', 'Running Footsteps', 'The Dog Wants His Dinner', 'The Crystal Lithium', 'Janis Joplin's Dead: Long Live Pearl', 'Eyes', 'The Night', 'Letter Poem #2'. Grateful acknowledgement is due to the author and the publishers for permission to include these poems.

KENWARD ELMSLIE

Circus Nerves and Worries

When that everybody's legal twin Mrs Trio
enters the casino, I expect personal disaster.
Out of next winter's worst blizzard I'm convinced
into the lobby and up the ladder she'll hustle
holding that squeaky velvet purse to one ear.
Placing one green and black peppermint-striped chip
gingerly on zero, zero it is. Which is when I fall dead.
In my shower while soaping. This very next year.

Goony intuition? Well, once in April at the Cafe Jolie
pointblank she asked: this terror at time in your eyes,
wouldn't crossing a river help? How about now?
Give up my innocence hunt, I exclaimed,
intimacies with failure, all my 'sudden magic' hopes?
And today came this dream about moths, I lied,
mouthing, yes wisdoms. Only how to read their lips?
    Tell me! Tell me!
I dream about vines, she said. Thank you and *ciao*.

Yesterday I looked at my body. Fairly white.
Today fairly white, the same. No betterment.
Why can't I feel air? Or take in mountains?
I lose my temper at pine needles, such small stabs.
Breezes scratch me (different from feeling)
and I long to breathe water. Agenda tomorrow:
cable her care of casino TIME TERROR GONE
STOP SEAWEED DREAM GREAT STOP
    (actually, a lie).

Ancestor Worship

They advanced towards Point A,
their malicious grandfather. What a purposeful safari:
    sundry treaties,
    water rights, the key to the code to be firmed.

A trail of their old kid gloves
hurled at ferns – any green branch, grrr – did beckon them
    back.
    How often fronds, let go too soon, slashed their
    cheeks!

Deeper they fled and soon their blond wrist hair,
as if from boyish match tricks, frizzled and curled,
    charred by the spike-like ping of the jungle wind.

Their gifts were devoured, the weeklies by beetles,
rendering any new stance for Point A impossible. Ants
    chomped at
    the jigsaw puzzles, ground with their hideous
    mandibles

treey landscapes and Venices at sunset, crunched at
gift vitamin packages, mobile replicas of lares and penates,
    gaunt and swinging, all for Point A,

chomped and chomped up their changes of clothes,
now three four five sizes too big, why? Why? WHY?
    Continued next week?
    No one could eat or sleep or complete

the act of love, so mostly they discussed
their new diseases, compared hallucinations. The young
    master
    coughed himself inside out one day, and bravo!

rematerialized as a red cactus, with string growths.
The bearers hooted, one by one vanished when new maps
     brought out
   proved Point A was only a waterfall

   behind which grandfather sat naked and cooled,
singing of traffic organized like a factory, rashly.
     On heavy afternoons, monkeys brought the group
     tidbits,

   litters tilted so, forming a shelter against rain,
and the group'd perform, wedging themselves like vines,
     leaves, wet
   flowers, into a swampy pattern so inanimate

   they fooled even the leanest panthers. One day they
     agreed
Point A was a mine full of tunnels here and there. How
     giant insects are
   they noticed too late and only then, poor remnants.

Fringe People

For Ruth Yorck

How to tell fringe people from yourself, himself, us, you,
    her?
They hunt for clean central beds full of lovers to deceive.
When they enter rooms, the most valuable still-life shatters.
They scream 'Trap!', deliberately trip (won't get up, ever
    leave).

Thus their Hollywood looks get damaged. Forced to aim at
Invisibility, they hide for hours, hood for weeks. Oops
    there they are!
Caught pulling at their lips, they form the Pro-Compassion
    League.
Dreadful clowns, their motto: for every laugh a scar.

Their latest? 'Get centered is our this year's mystique,
Our ideal of haven is a hurricane's eye, a calm norm
And to hell with the others!' Verbatim. Alas their mask
Even inches away looks like perfect skin and their smile,
    ah warm.

Communique for Orpheus

My Army   likes you so much. The young cadets
               in their handsome yellow boots
               and kepis and sashes . . .

My Army   how to explain, my very own Army,
               the orderlies, the nurses, the countermen,
               the laundresses, their new silence?

My Army   loves you I think. Whether they be pursers,
               mechanics, eye doctors, night watchmen,
               those iron-faced officers . . .

My Army   feels sick today. The men are all grumbling,
               they want to join your side – you! – and then
               celebrate victory with fireworks and parades.
               They request a photo of your singing voice
               for the imminent fireworks and parades.
               Candies of you are welcome in case of
               fireworks and parades, as are any movies
               of you yourself chewing smiling etc.
               even sleeping etc. for the about-to-commence
               fireworks and parades.

               *   *   *

               'His whole army is infatuated, infatuated.
               A silly god rose out of the sea, made out
               of sexy tin with bandages here and there
               and it makes hitherto unheard-of sounds,
               and changes into man, woman, God, money,
               disease, social justice, Beauty – at will!
               Benjamin Franklin has a sick headache.

O where is the country heading, and what
can I, a mere man, do?'
                                        – George Washington

*　　*　　*

My Army   likes you so much. The young cadets
          in their handsome yellow boots
          and kepis and sashes
          call you obscenities softly. Dedicated?
          There is no raillery in the latrines,
          and in their sleep they moan
          madonna madonna.

My Army   loves you I think. At strategy conferences,
          those iron-faced officers thrash out
          memories of your tinniest sounds.
          Tears fall on crucial mountains.
          Dilemmas of survival . . .

*　　*　　*

'I hear the sound of mandolins. Let me
fly away with you.'
                                        – Theodore Roosevelt

*　　*　　*

My Army   keeps busy.
          Man 20 feet. Man 20 feet. Man 20 feet.
          Guarding pipelines from desert area to
          industrial complex.
          Testing sirens, scrubbing sirens, painting
              sirens,
          guarding the oils and gases necessary
          for the siren system, and so the years
          pass and pass.

My Army   likes you so much.
If state secrets arrive
(in food, lightbulbs, street refuse)
thank the spies.
Who vie with each other for blueprints.
Who envy the corridor-like structure
of your chicaneries.
Who despise all who can hear your voice
in the threshing machines,
the mid-day boiler explosions,
the violin rallies.

*   *   *

'An enemy trick rose out of the sea,
and his whole army went swimming.
Phooey. Bronze somersaults. Tonight
they returned in silence. Hellish bivouac,
blast the tom-toms. Meanwhile the animals
thump and wheeze, circling round our tiny
encampment, and the birds with their red
beaks screech and screech, and I wonder
how long can I keep the capitol inviolate?'
           – Douglas MacArthur

*   *   *

My Army   loves you I think.
But for fun it takes bus expeditions
through the colossal Ice Zoo.
Perfectly preserved, two black pumas
locked in mortal combat. Two penguins
locked in mortal combat. Perfectly preserved
monkeys and birds, long extinct species,
perfectly preserved, each in its own ice
    segment,

locked in mortal combat, perfectly pre-
    served.
O dirty bus windows, let them see out!

My Army   sends you this historic painting
'Painting of You' ...
BOOM!

My Army   likes you so much
loves you I think so much
they are marching to your hit recording *Me*!
Hurry, when will *Us* be released?
Panic is spreading, what will it sound like?
A bleep, a sobby kid, two whole peoples?
How to know, how to know.
Hurry, is it smashed,
help, where is it? Help!
They my army wants to shout
hello into your navel
(Help!) and hear that old song
(Help!) come out to explain
(Help!) the seasons
(Help!) harvests
(Help!) plus certain facts about storms that
    start
(Help!) (Help!) on the (They can kill!)
    moon.

Nov 25

toy bird on its back one metal wing now broken
once tottered tempo arthritic spastic

along an El sidewalk in a fifties home movie
featuring a clean-cut boy version of Ashbery

gazing sexily at sparrers in a gym with open windows
the express gathers momentum and now you see

Frank O'Hara walking on the tracks suiciding supposedly
John Latouche the bird's winder-upper died first

and soon after I turned into the 'baby poet'
inventor of the read-a curved pretzel ocean moon hands

a slight delay while the ribbon expands
the breakage around this desk is something fierce

dumb how the object all too often outlasts the person
all too often not counting art shoot why count art he
    gagged

a testy insight due to the aging process repeat aging process
skipping breakfast always put me in a confessional mood

frankly I began this poem day before yesterday
the title's a downright lie more so by the minute

especially as this poem's been festering let's see
since I lost that toy car in the black space under the house

my first memory (dirt) the victrola's running down
and that witch in the tree outside is waiting to strangle me

frankly this poem started to be about a photo Nov 25
Nixon's shoes being shined front-page Nov 25

two shoeshine boys bent way way down Nov 25
freak-out overtones of foot kissage

leading to clompy polkas of national ass lickage
of great beefy men on red leather thrones

in a marble station yellowed with – looks like
hippies have been dropping stuff on the cops again

the soft-drink industry must be ecstatic anyway
meanwhile us good guys are stalled in the Tunnel of Fuzz

'stuck my dong up the Great Speckled Hawg
them glinty shiny flecks was molybdenum zinc'

the lights just came on again all over the world
a slight decay while the ribbon gets some rest

some deep-freeze therapy for us women and kids please
and when we come back up and the tundra starts to fizz

with our secret oral teachings (psalm one: city lights)
we'll wrap our bombed friends in palm fronds

and become a singing people (did you enjoy your turkey)
hey we *are* a singing people (the wing part tasted metallic)

The Champ

Part I

A woozy clarity adorns all liars
like a photo of a friendly yes.
When their boots get patted in strategic places,
they leave jewels in trees (retouched)

and grow partial to shacks and torn sheets.
Each tired day (an orgy of clichés)
they meet demands, budge.
If a food at a Red Moon

flies up into the flue,
they demand, 'Alter the files:
Fat: Men's stares, tinsel,
pompous return of grandfather shell,

jettison peasant furniture into volcano,
set fire to his/her fortune.'
The cars in front of the hotel look dented.
When he comes, he of the red face, he must tell

his niece eying the thermometer
to defy the room. Get down to work.
Sleep alone, Horace – fall asleep fast!
Your evening lie amuses the fog –

waltzing, companions, clucks,
an old piece of cheese, distances,
the supper 'don'ts' which make one let go
if the Yankee would only finish his orange!

In the Allegheny Mountains, the grumpy terrain
rises up to the clouds methodically
and flares out like three noses shuddering.
Every winter, burros run amok among the tractors.

Riflemen return to their rooms.
Thus women poison their semen
and by a sort of cancerous jealousy jumble
the former wife, the shadows, passing cocoa,

the rooster, standing amid the rich chocolate.
Then snoring, they enter – conscripts in nightgowns
holding lamps. The purge begins at dawn.
A child crosses the dust to the basin.

He assassinates his mother, is born,
flowers. Perfume. Boredom. Asparagus.
The tree map smells of asparagus.
Ever find a coin in a church

covertly? It's like stepping on friends
(wheezing from obvious dreams) under newspapers.
Or like false teeth on a priest-pilot
who remembers his past – its yellowness –

as he walks, an old man with a knife in January.
The walls of Siena appeal most likely to his conscience
floating like Persian bats with the wind.
The archer represents a return to crime.

Always he's wished to be in accord with crime: crime
(that rectal thermometer)
excites his loins. Next door in the chain room,
Seurat's 'The Dutchmen' is kneeled to

by dadaists dressed as ninnies.
Why is the whip trial fire so expensive?
Nerves fray easily in the Rouge Capitol.
The comings and goings are unsatisfactory – cellulose

stinks of all the numbers in the soil.
Side by side, little hills grrr
to win the Grand Prize given by the courtesan.
If (in practice) she climbs onto a man in a long circle,

and puts her legs around him like Joan of Arc,
he will be next in line to rule the caravan –
if, if the bossy wind touches his booth.
And if the pretext of a penchant for confiscated bags

doubles his pleasure in reading the poems
'Ancient Astronomer' and 'Yes Cakes'.
From the zodiac, one'll puzzle out the scene.
Hot milk tidied up the attendant's pot.

'Old males,' St Martin says, 'have their summer
made possible by being and having summer.'
'An architect obsessed by gates grows larger
than an explorer who takes himself for a street urchin.'

'A theologian who sees the Virgin in her filth
becomes a celebrity more or less because of her filth.'
'A tic prompted by a trussed up fish
is worth more than a beautiful teenager's shush.'

Gyres sang in the cup like pearly choirs.
An osier of elaborate cereal figured in the purge –
authorities have no sense of dramaturgy.
That's how it goes. Children enslave sleep

so the core of the past is in their mouths.
Their only creed is strawberries,
and when ogres in big boots appear,
no bottles whisper of death's return.

Still and all, old males compose suicide notes
and wall themselves up one way or another.
'The president who points to a bruised olive
signs his dispatches with saliva.'

Such lush excuses endanger bon vivants,
soup reporters and wolves.
To whom sell the boots?
The inheritor of the pendant: the corpse.

The pool, how, the egg she pondered,
the egg of the dog she has foundered –
how ignorant to see 'verse' in a big boat
from which mature fragments emerge

as if this squalid world were a pasture.
'What are these warm words,' said the girl in the train.
Her aunt knew she had never sampled
morphine, lovers, the 'kill' ring, happy cures,

classified pleasures located on a queer peak
(ecstatic mountain-climbers at the edge of a crevasse
know how the universe . . . for rent . . .)
where to a bird, the suffocating sun is like marble.

In July, she dined with a man under a tree, his tree,
and his napkin dropped, and too far to be reached.
Her memory of strawberries sang, sang
while he looked for the wafer-white moon at noon

walking away, his head askew, a man
moving like a fly on a slow-moving train.
Richard's torso had been ornate with bacon,
a carafe in search of a little mouth.

Familiars streaked down the female road.
Once a year, merely part of the carnival,
horses caught sight of the writing,
and thinking they were on fire, refused to climb down.

In front, the cretin played with a cinder.
Deliberately, lunch-time rolled around –
a ragout without comparison in the whole pass.
Towards the rate-payers, a singular parade

of horses brushed the air without displacing one cinder.
Pure song issued from the illustrations of claws,
trilling appropriate to such an energetic locale.
How eccentric! The same accent as John's son

Bull the Clown, who narrated 'The Pistol Sky',
testing each final point on his tongue
(clear seeds in a dry cascade become amply big peas):
'The Jockey with big feet has a hundred books.

He thinks there is a beauty in his family, walled up,
who can no longer hear the murmur of the mountains
since – in the plaque – mother turned into sister – ' . . .
Rented cars on the move are as artistic as rolling stairways.

Racers, drunks, mazes, downtown branches,
the nation is hysterical. Frustrated cathodes,
the fire of Dutchmen, the original battering rams,
have been replaced by charred dolls, under a permanent
    sun, dry.

Revolutionary Letter

The pulp magazine lay there, dangling sloppily, two-thirds etc. Flat etc. piled high etc. with typically ugly etc. New Jersey roadside situation etc. In the fissures cockroaches were peering out, lined up to enjoy the sunrise and the distant orange-flecked towers of the futuristic city. All chunked out in an obvious way – irregular shapes, linear in a tilty way – all chunked out in an obvious way. Just what'd appeal to the stenographer clomping around in wedgies, fidgeting with her baby-pink snood with one hand, and with the other trying to finish the orange popsicle before it melts in the sun. What a tell-tale trail on the side-walk: it skirts the pale blue plastic doily with the marzipan of the trumpet hearing aid centered on it, on the curb next to the person on the stretcher in the gutter surrounded by young people in green smocks – trainees probably. The stenographer is shouting at her, time for the news and the weather, please come home! The orange liquid has wetted the doily. The person's fingers are so agitated! Sign language? One of the smock people is interpreting: pro-ceed to the corner, garden apartment, the newspaper, walk back to her griddle, potato pancakes, sticky fingers from maple syrup. She can't stand sticky fingers, but the inferior paper napkins sold nowadays shred easily, and however patient and careful one may start out being, one is soon sawing the air with abrasive gestures, surely the inter-preter is elaborating somewhat – the person has a good, simple face, though its spirituality may be accented by the closed eyes. The interpreter is shouting about 'blocks' etc. 'Lumps.' 'Excess material cluttering up the new de-clivities, it's so rusty from the increasingly difficult to predict storm patterns, one can't move them into sheltered areas due to the snarled mobility sequences ... nothing

goes by . . . the metal piece must be moved ten yards . . .
serrated edges that can do unquestionable physical damage
. . . a veritable onrush . . . dyed blonde harridans with baby
carriages laden with groceries . . . big meaty men in vicuna
coats forming a flying wedge' . . . 'lumps.' He simply refuses
to say the word 'chunks' – all chunked out in an obvious
way – irregular shapes, linear in a tilty way – all chunked
out in an obvious way. So obvious!

Paper Suns

Gordon makes abusive telephone calls. Uncle Charles pulls
over to the side by an inn. He gets out of the car and dies.
Gordon comes to the funeral and walks in the garden but
does not set foot in the house. Ken takes up the crusade!
He avoids introducing her to his future wife. She sends
two chairs as a wedding present. Mervin thinks that with
so much china in her house, she should write him – use all
you want, take all you want. His partner is killed in the war.
The papers proving ownership of the properties has been
transferred are lost. The money is totally lost. Bill goes to a
prep school where he wins scholarships. From there, to
Cambridge, where he studies law. He is hired out to an
agency as a tutor. He forgets to take his name off the rolls!
He goes to Paris with a money-belt strapped around his
waist. The yacht sets sail and turns around in mid-stream.
Land boom in Canada! He goes there. He becomes a useful
foil. Edith whirls from one diplomat to another and uses
him to keep off too ardent swains. He is an eccentric who
really is not eccentric. He never quite makes a go of his
life. Some people lose sizable sums, which he never pays
back or regards as his fault. He quarrels and goes off to
make munitions. To be on his own? To do something for
his country? The banks fold. 'Where shall we eat, honey?'
Mary bets Bill that Constance's five dollar gold-piece will
not be accepted. On a hillside, he says, 'We'll make you
manageress.' She asks Constance if he's serious. Constance
says, 'Oh no. It only gives him something to talk about.'
She spends hours on the phone. Alice and Mary come over.
Gordon moves. Kenward won't go on the same train. He
gets up earlier and comes home later. This goes on for a
year. 'Why not let him make his own friends, lead his own

life?' 'The money, I haven't the money.' Doris never signs a check. Once a week she accounts for everything spent. Ken goes to Nigeria. He begins to die. He never gets over the shock. Something is knocked out of him.

White Attic

The white attic rests
among dripping trees

with unrolling tunnels
and trembling luggage

around were dens
all kinds of dens

and dazzling fruit
to weary the wind

the sun would end
and we'd smoke among the trees

our wary arms
tenderly relaxed

the urn faces a tree
of unequal height

when it came I grew
moved to two rooms in town

where I reach out at night
and bat the far air

Japanese City

Centennial of Melville's birth this morning.
Whale balloons drift up released by priests. Whale floats
    parade
followed by boats of boys in sou'westers jiggled by runners
followed by aldermen in a ritual skiff propelled by 'surf' –
    girls.
In my hotel room with its cellophane partitions (under-
    watery)
I phone down for ice-water, glass, tumbler, and the cubes.

Cattle for the Xmas Market fill the streets.
Black snouts – a rubby day indeed. Bump the buildings,
    herds.
A Mexican seamstress brings back my underthings shyly
six, seven times a day. One sweats so, lying about.
She mentions marvelous pistachio green caverns
where one canoes through cool midgy Buddha beards

where drafts of polar air sound like cicadas, where –
About the partitions. The other travellers seem –
There were beautiful hairs in the wash-basin this A.M. –
thick, and they smelled of limes
(good, that jibes with mine – ugh! –)
but mine, how perverse! Form a hoop, you there. Mine,

mine smell like old apples in a drawer. Jim the Salesman
and his cohorts are massaging my feet – a real treadmill
    example.
They're in lawn decor, ether machines, and nocturnal
    learning clasps.

And Jim? Plays cards in his shorts, moves black fish
    around.
Black houses, the capitol. Hotel chunks. Sky chunks. The
    squeeze:
green odd numbers – white air, amputations and eagles,
    respite.
Red even numbers – body sections, the ocean sac, the great
    beach.
Green even numbers – oval jewels, quicksand, the haven
    behind the falls.
Jim's stammer is contagious, zen smut about hatcheries in
    the suburbs,
how the women in the canneries came down with the
    'gills',
hence bathtub love-makings, couplings in the sewers. The
    ice-water comes.

The room-clerk's pate shines up through the transparent
    floor.
Soon the sin couples will start arriving, and the one-way
    mirror teams
and the government professionals with their portable
    amulets –
shiny vinyl instruments that probe and stretch.
Much visiting back and forth. Pink blobs. Revels and
    surveys.
Many olive eyes'll close in a sleep of exhaustion. More ice-
    water!

The celebrants in metal regalia jangle and tinkle
moving past the red-roofed villas of the Generals,
past the cubicles of the nakeds and into the harbor,
past the glum stone busts of the Generals, sitting in the
    water.

Out they go, (Jim etc.) into the sweet emptied city, leaving
   behind
the red odd numbers untouched: pleasure beaches, mon-
   soons and sun.

Shirley Temple Surrounded by Lions

In a world where kapok on a sidewalk looks like an
    'accident'
– innards – would that freckles could enlarge, well,
    meaningfully
into kind of friendly brown kingdoms, all isolate,
with a hero's route, feral glens,
    and a fountain where heroines cool their mouths.

Scenario: an albino industrialiste, invited to the beach
    at noon
(and to such old exiles, oceans hardly teem with ambigui-
    ties)
by a lifeguard after her formulae, though in love –
'Prop-men, the gardenias, the mimosa need anti-droopage
    stuffing.'
Interestingly slow, the bush and rush filming.

Hiatus, everyone. After the idea of California sort of took
    root,
we found ourselves in this cookie forest; she closed the
    newspaper,
groped past cabañas, blanched and ungainly.

The grips watched Marv and Herm movies of birds
    tweeting,
fluttering around and in and out an old boat fridge, on a
    reef,
when eek, the door – or was it 'eef' – 'Shirl' said the
    starling, end of –

The janitors are watching movies of men and women
   ruminating.
Then a cartoon of two clocks, licking. Chime. Licking,
   chime. *Then* a?
   After that, photos of incinerators in use moved families
      more than
the candy grass toy that retches. Dogs. For the dressers,
   'Mutations',
   about various feelers. For the extras, movies of revenge
      that last.

This spree *has* to last. 'Accept my pink eyes, continual
   swathing,'
Shirley rehearsed. 'Encase me in sand, then let's get kissy.'
   Do children have integrity, i.e. eyes? Newsreels, ponder
      this.
How slow the filming is for a grayish day with its bonnet
   bumping along the pioneer footpath, pulled by – here,
   yowly hound.

Feathered Dancers

Inside the lunchroom the travelling nuns wove
sleeping babies on doilies of lace.
A lovely recluse jabbered of bird lore and love:
                    'Sunlight tints my face

                    and warms the eggs outside
                    perched on filthy columns of guilt.
                    In the matted shadows where I hide,
                    buzzards moult and weeds wilt.'

Which reminds me of Mozambique
in that movie where blacks massacre Arabs.
The airport runway (the plane never lands, skims off) is
    bleak –
scarred syphilitic landscape – crater-sized scabs –

painted over with Pepsi ads –
as in my lunar Sahara dream – giant net comes out of sky,
encloses my open touring car. Joe slumps against Dad's
emergency wheel turner. Everyone's mouth-roof dry.

One interpretation. Mother hated blood!
When the duck Dad shot dripped on her leatherette lap-
    robe,
dark spots not unlike Georgia up-country mud,
her thumb and forefinger tightened (karma?) on my ear-
    lobe.

Another interpretation. Motor of my heart stalled!
I've heard truckers stick ping-pong balls up their butt
and jounce along having coast-to-coast orgasms, so called.
Fermés, tousled jardins du Far West, I was taught – tight
    shut.

– 38 –

So you can't blame them. Take heed, turnpikes.
Wedgies float back from reefs made of jeeps: more offshore
   debris.
Wadded chewy depressants and elatants gum up footpaths.
   Remember Ike's
'Doctor-the-pump-and-away-we-jump' Aloha Speech to
   the Teamsters? 'The – '

he began and the platform collapsed, tipping him onto a
   traffic island.
An aroused citizenry fanned out through the factories that
   day
to expose the Big Cheese behind the sortie. Tanned,
I set sail for the coast, down the Erie and away,

and ate a big cheese in a café by the docks,
and pictured every room I'd ever slept in:
toilets and phone-calls and oceans. Big rocks
were being loaded, just the color of my skin,

and I've been travelling ever since,
so let's go find an open glade,
like the ones in sporting prints,
(betrayed, delayed, afraid)

where we'll lie among the air-plants
in a perfect amphitheatre in a soft pink afterglow.
How those handsome birds can prance,
ah . . . unattainable tableau.

Let's scratch the ground clean,
remove all stones and trash,
I mean open dance-halls in the forest, I mean
where the earth's packed smooth and hard. Crash!

It's the Tale of the Creation. The whip cracks.
Albatrosses settle on swaying weeds.
Outside the lunchroom, tufts and air-sacs
swell to the size of fruits bursting with seeds.

Night Soil

Wrestled with smudges to attain the solar sheen you crave.
No reason in particular, except your wake-up wince,
and when you squint, can't see that violet network radiating
            outward
            (favorite childhood city) (eyeball) (rapid transit)
            (drugged caper of spaced-out spider) (Chicago)
            (flashlight suspended from ceiling) (euphoria hub)
which gives that feeling of well-being that means business
            is good.

Harangue: a new sky glares at us,
perforated by some authority or other's scent nozzles.
Perennial emergency, fuck off!
Then something South of France-ish to taper off to,
lemon verbena sifting down.
Rancid. Muttered: rancid.

Fledglings clomp about on the fire-escapes,
fire-escapes leading to and from silly heights,
heights designed to crumple inside a bag filled with lunar
            air,
air that insures perpetual nights with lots of sterile glitter.
Thus non-seeing organisms can really relax and trust stuff,
even the sodden slap slap slap of ephemera battling to get
            in,
persistent as a lazy lagoon bespangled orange twice a day,
orange as those distant relations, half-seen, half-sieve,
who don't realize how low the lowlands are,
lowlands that vent a dapper dullness,
the epitome of summer's end.

Warm farm weather's tarnishing the sky this time.
I love it when weather's like a speedboat in a lucky scene
in which pieces bob along, having perky tantrums,
tantrums because that windbreaker's zipper's a speck,
but if the light turns orange again,
it may be it's a lane
leading tractor onto plane.

Mere nostrums in the dusty brains of rusty men,
ready to leave these binds, egged on by a dogged with-it
    feeling,
feeling that a chunk of wood under dried grass (under
    snow)
by dint of sheer mattedness culls from the shadows
shadows that bounce from stone to stone.

A distant waterfall dumps rumblings on deaf lovers,
dear lovers, dead lovers. Rainy season's begun.

At entrance, pensioner sips beer. Little prissy thoughts.
Sneaky gas tamps down too-too raunchy udder draughts.
Another epitome of summer's end.

Another epitome of summer's end:
laser beams accelerating in operating rooms
papered over with derisive in-a-puny-time tits,
atchoo, atchoo, they fly shrieking into the air,
darkening the sky like a rain cloud
just to scratch some no longer obscene epithet on the one
                source of light,
as one might dirty a swank motel-room's white ruthlessness
till the last temporary wall has made itself scarce.

Jan 24

for John Ashbery –

take care keep in touch best wish for New Year
what'll it be: tango palace in banana republic

that's one of the luxuries of longish-term survival in
   NYC
thinking of smallness and walled-off sad little dumb little
   places

New Zealand was my first post-puberty country crush
how it welcomed me and my wonderful labor-saving
   devices

permanent waves strap-onable wings automats for the
   capitol
socialism I love you your housing weekends sandy-lashed
   settlers

first let me explain my 'just room for one more' dread
picture book of World War I mounds of about-to-be-
   buried corpses

sub-sub-sub basement flashed by hours ago and still moving
   down
that fu manchu creep peering through the peep-hole is no
   super

judging from the lamasery teetering on the fez-strewn
   cornice
it's Albania and I'm to rescue poor dear dotty King Zog

milk-white victim hands are protruding out of the glacier
    below
hands that sprout bushy werewolf hair when the moon is
    full

electrolysis and gelatine capsules could keep these hands
    nice
the catch is the nation's lovelies'd grow freak mustaches

the clandestine crystal set lights up: you're #1 Commie, Anna
it's Roumania and Anna Pauker pushes off in the goat-cart

polemics polemics polemics she moans phuffle phuffle sigh
my first lady dictator whew that explains the butch hair-do

lucky she has me to brain the transmission key
in mid-enzyme-synthetic-organ-introjection hormone cycle

Anna wake up the transmission key is now smashed
Anna and Zog are playing bezique on the Blue Express

dance manual *pour moi*? Anna rests her scruffy head on his
    shoulder
a solitary tear wends its errant way skirting medal after
    medal

piranha are nibbling iron clouds above Tirana
their droppings – filings – scoot about the cobblestones

magnetized by distant word reverberations (memo: keep
    ears to ground)
back to Anna and Zog in their sumptuous berth (Praha
    München Paris)

see the green cube Anna in the mesh cooker unit
it's poking out its pterodactyl wings very over-soul, hein?

its beak is caught Anna says taking hammer from handbag
it's probing its feathers for social parasites like us Zog
    joshes

Papillons d'amour Anna says swooning into a spoon position
her first dirty joke and they awoke thus in a bus in the
    Rockies

just as this morning we awoke in a spoon position you and I
unfolded unthinkingly and dispersed for another time's up
    type day

Motor Disturbance

Could be inching my way across moth turbulence
(wrong country? Honduras? – No! No! Nepal!)
due to a motor disturbance in some itinerary program com-
   puter
that failed to take into account my aversion to hot weather
   decay

and my love of eternal white silence
the result of a motor disturbance on some solar slope
I keep sliding down thanks to my own personal motor
   disturbance
the one that makes me puff up and screech (dog stars)

when I'd rather celebrate a White Cliff Mass
with friendly co-innocents in a clean commune above the
   clouds
where I won't have to cerebrate how to – how to – rip up
   stuff
work-oriented ancients painstakingly mass-produced

in vast sheets of legible shimmering matter
inspired, don't you know, by a longitude-latitude motor
   disturbance
(Earth plunges into new electro-magnetic black space
   field) –
exhausting! I can't control my current motor disturbance –

so clicky, soppy, so picky – like the one that led me to
   assume
'disfunction' was Brooklynese for 'wedding' (nervous
   laughter)
which prompted me to dial NERVOUS first thing today
seeing as my booster clock . . . burnt oasis . . . plastic goo

so much of it this time of – of –
the operator's voice was laden with irony
irony I have no time to savor
due to the motor disturbance of this end-of-year period

which seems to be hurtling down a sleety dynamo
throbbing with hallucinatory instructions
each syllable of which lasts out a year of its own choosing
thanks to a blessed motor disturbance in the Heavens

i.e. your lips, gills, hills, tips –
a very contemporary motor disturbance as gorgeous as
    blue plates
spinning and wobbling and falling
conjoining to form Sky, replacing the old peeling one . . .

Sometimes you must persevere in the face of a huge motor
    disturbance
that settles on a whole city's brain like a big black bowl
part of an everywhere-in-the-universe night
like the one I see when the two mountains wrestling each
    other lie down

which happened in my mind just as I careened into your
    arms by mistake
to wish you a half-gnawed ear (new motor disturbance, I
    hate you!)
to wish you a Happy New Year Times (got it right for
    once)
and Happy New Year Times is my favorite motor dis-
    turbance of all

next to you who can transform stalled traffic into a beautiful
    panora –
(never get to finish this word in this particular lifetime)
ma – ma – a mama of endless blinky fields
with unicorns that honk as they twine around each other
    with langorous etc.

thanks to a permanent motor disturbance
just like mine, like yours, like ours, like our ecstasy
the ecstasy we left our nation in our will
to help it shudder its way through its inventive mole-run

the one its machines invented due to their one great motor
    disturbance,
the one that was supposed to prevent all the others,
the others that make me unable to figure out why
there's not one motor disturbance in the January sky

and in the winter air
with you there
everything in my life just seems to jell,
farewell.

Chinese Creep

for Harry Mathews

Reading Railroad. Gives a sigh
twice a day. Twice a day.

Gas girls, a set of hymns
dancing on the ceiling.

Precious little palaver.
Clean lion enters.

Cuss calls out to hoss: 'Monument!'
Two minutes wait minute Two.

Shadowy nickels and quarters and dimes –
the big stiff.

Drastic variables:
so much lava, Fatso.

Rose. Then rose-colored. It's the Chinese Creep,
shadowy as the room into which he merges.

Clamber into your ump apparel fast.
Tring! Don't smell the bed, Bub.

Feel small and bombed today: lenient.
Liable to spell

last breath
fast birth.

An ominous gritting of the teeth
gumbo in a dirigible

thought he said: attack of miasma.
Referring to my asthma.

Damn mess.
In the stratosphere, same old fakery.

Reading Railroad, sometimes stresses
are afraid to wait too long – they get fizzy.

Then I feel loved in the altogether,
then I mean business. You get engaged, wham,

it's so precarious. Rose-colored liquids
redden the rain, Tlooth liquids.

Tlooth. Tlooth.
Scleam. Scleam.

No one will hear you but the hungly lats.
Something for which there's no sob-sister.

So much exhaust in this mattress.
In this pillow, silent stone hair.

Girl Machine

my nerves my nerves I'm going mad
my nerves my nerves I'm going mad
            round-the-world
                hook-ups
head lit up   head lit up   head lit up
            the fitting, the poodle
Ma Marine   Ma Marine   Ma Marine
Ma Marine   Ma Marine   Ma Marine
            the fitting, the poodle

what a life,   just falling in and out of
what a life,   just falling in and out of
            swimming pools
zylophones   WANTED   zylophones
WANTED   female singer   WANTED
bigtime   floorshow   bigtime   floorshow
bigtime   floorshow   bigtime   floorshow
            silhouetted in
                moonlight
                moonlight

            mysterious mirrors
            mysterious mirrors
            mysterious mirrors

Louella Parsons

swell teeth	not news	swell teeth
'woo-woo'	woo-woo	'woo-woo'
vaccinated at	6 o'clock in	San Die
vaccinated at	6 o'clock in	San Die
'woo-woo'	woo-woo	'woo-woo'
swell teeth	not news	swell teeth

Louella Parsons

shiny black surfaces
shiny black surfaces
shiny black surfaces

head lit up	head lit up	head lit up
	a girl machine	
	a girl machine	
head lit up	head lit up	head lit up

work work work   work work work
work work work   work work work
work work work   work work work
work work work   work work work

GIRL MACHINE GIRL MACHINE
GIRL MACHINE GIRL MACHINE
GIRL MACHINE GIRL MACHINE

'Busby Berkely is the only film dir
'Busby Berkely is the only film dir
to have fully experienced and re
to have fully experienced and re
Babe Rainbow Babe Rainbow
Babe Rainbow Babe Rainbow
signed Kenward G. Elms
signed Kenward G. Elms
mirrors provide a 2-
mirrors provide a 2-
for-1 opulence (D
for-1 opulence (D
epression /flo
epression /flo
wers: shit
wers: shit

wers: shit
wers: shit
on from above
on from above
bunches unfolding
bunches unfolding
in his 'Footlight Par
in his 'Footlight Par
signed Kenward G. Elms
signed Kenward G. Elms
Babe Rainbow Babe Rainbow
Babe Rainbow Babe Rainbow
beautiful people working for us!!
beautiful people working for us!!
'Busby Berkely is the only film dir
'Busby Berkely is the only film dir

GIRL MACHINE GIRL MACHINE
GIRL MACHINE GIRL MACHINE
GIRL MACHINE GIRL MACHINE

show   gets   on   and   is   a   smasheroo
show   gets   on   and   is   a   smasheroo
                round-the-world
                    hook-ups
head lit up   head lit up   head lit up
head lit up   head lit up   head lit up
    Ruby   Ruby
            col 'yum' nist
(1969)   BABE RAINBOW   (1969)
            a girl machine
        reflected and refracted
by   black   floors   &   mystery   meers
by   black   floors   &   mystery   meers
Night in Shanghai Night in Shanghai

GIRL MACHINE GIRL MACHINE
GIRL MACHINE GIRL MACHINE
GIRL MACHINE GIRL MACHINE

lips painted red   lips painted red
keep on doing it   keep on doing it
      the oriental fans part
distant hands . .   . . distant hands
they come nearer   they come nearer
harmonica player   harmonica player
     creepy Chink beggars
whores kiss Dick   whores kiss Dick
falls for Jane Wy   falls for Jane Wy
pursued by gangs   pursued by gangs
     carries her shot dead
down a shadowy endless Dream Corridor!
harmonica player   harmonica player
they get smaller!   they get smaller!
distant hands . .   . . distant hands
     the oriental fans close

      42nd St.   42nd St.
      42nd St.   42nd St.
     reflected and refracted
by   black   floors   and   mystery   meers
     reflected and refracted
      42nd St.   42nd St.
      42nd St.   42nd St.

you   in   the   view   and   no   real   walls
you   in   the   view   and   no   real   walls
express flow   black-whi
express flow   black-whi
            firm shiny terror
            firm shiny terror
express flow   black-whi
express flow   black-whi
you   in   the   view   and   no   real   walls
you   in   the   view   and   no   real   walls

GIRL MACHINE. GIRL MACHINE.
GIRL MACHINE. GIRL MACHINE.
GIRL MACHINE. GIRL MACHINE.

                  bunches
              like   flowers
down the ramp   down the ramp
happy factory   happy factory
just relax   just relax

Ground Hog Day Pensée

... hands to the ranting parents, mosquito parents un-accustomed to so much dancing air (mental block) – flee into their glacier bombs in terror. Very air is dancing as it's zoned now, and it bestows kisses on the Mayor. The reeling skyscrapers (mental block) – gila monsters in the bushes fence in their own crazies and wishy-washies ...

Shaddap. It's daytime, and identical phrases are going to start to come out of mouths, which'll keep everything peaceful, peaceful and strange.

Hand

The hand, wizened but sprightly, circled the round tool-shed, hunting for Romulus and Remus in what it took to be the total chaos of Outer Space. The dissonance that sounded like time moving backwards, faster and faster, was actually the racket some pals of the Dawn Brigade (out scrounging for circuits) were making, hurling hard balls of mica at zombies (this is what's so ironic) – victims of amnesia (this is what's so ironic) but elephant-sized, standing in the endless swamp.

Eventual Bruises

Adventurers of yesteryear are working their way deeper into ravines where lie Baby's toy bikes in Baby's footlockers: a veritable oasis. A major pleasure to act sappy, with a gracious lack of commitment (last one left) as one speeds along an underground river, soaping one's naked body in the comparative gloom – that's real poise. Clicking dials meet clicking dials. The dry river bed smells like farts, which is a sure sign to the dials the little white stones must be eggs that'll never hatch.

Air

sight
impinges
on air

divvying it up
(night sky)
into a cup

black earth
(good omen)
full of mica

suspended overhead
it's July
I'm full of joy

no steam heat
no cream teat
no dream meat

just walking around
watching the cup
dump its load

right on my head
cool black jelly
full of glints

hints
to remind me
of air

Tropicalism

1

Ate orange.
Legs stained . . . stains turn into fur patches . . . fur patches
turn into puma hide . . . palaver re escape route . . . boy's
lips . . . chicken feather along outer perimeter of lower
redder one, with up-and-down wrinkles . . . too much
pursing . . . spooky profiles peer sideways on high-rise
balconies . . . just dummies so the gov't'll think everyone's
home.

2

More palaver: ante-bellum. One lays one's smock on the
griffin. Siesta after a Technician Feast of foie gras, washed
down with Grapette. Siesta leaning against the Michelangelo Adam – cold muscles against which one rubs – no
guards to be afraid of. Gosh, how did they trundle them
here? Via those new erosion lines, along the orange-red
rivulets coursing beside the highway. Clump of bad-
mannered executives from the south, i.e. 'north' by your
mental gymnastics, but a fresh new north, full of fresh
new . . . executives . . . from even further north . . . they
really model themselves on penguins . . . experts at survival
. . . waiting under trees with leaves that hang down like
exhausted elephant ears, waiting for the rain to stop so they
can motion for the flotilla disguised as a parrot parade
float, with its ack-ack measles pellets that sound like someone sucking a stone teat. Ack-ack! Ack-ack!

3

Just have to wait till the situation is more 'human'. Coated with mud, massive anxiety attacks: vapors, zinc, can of *petit pois*, zinc, vapors. In the steam-room, a friendly Texan haw-haw, iced drinks sent in, two pink pillows with flamingo feathers inside, everyone oils up, and there's a lot of give-and-take (Embassy jerks) about lore.

4

They have two white-leaved vines twining around the Warrior Tree, which the men ingest the bark of, daily, thereby ingesting stren't. Also killing tree. When tree dies, so does Chief. Walks off into jungle. Some dress up in womanish fur-pieces, secrete beads under rock, join up with neighboring tribe as Chief's 'priestess-bride'. No one can touch priestess privates, real bad magic to see his dong. Doesn't exist. So, he has pick of women – that's really something: guilt mechanisms just don't function non-screwball way. So, he has pick of women. Chief's duty to fuck him up ass. While this, he is (belief) in trance communion state with this place's Warrior Tree, knows whether to attack other tribes or not, how, when. Say he says: ATTACK! So, they do. Victory! Metamorphosis: he becomes Chief's twin. Eventually, that means trouble. One-to-one fight, using two sticks. Poison on one end of one stick. Up to resident Chief's #1 Wife to hand out sticks. If she digs new Chief Twin he's in like Flynn. Poison by the way not fatal. In fact it's leaf-drug which elevates defeated chief into magic state: fly like bird, swim like fish, climb vines like fast bug. Ends his days revered Prophet. Food and love offerings daily, as he sits cross-legged at door of his stilt hut. Dies. Carried to top of Warrior Tree by youths and pulleys and basket of Eternity & Rain set in raft made of pelts tied to balsa, and there: set on fire. Ashes eaten by entire tribe, one speck or flake per person, wrapped in raw vine leaves. Two new vines planted by Resident Chief. Time begins again. Year One.

5

... but ice is like a ray sleeping ... I sobered up to certain pesky circumstances. How to stave off the hierarchic patterns that really maim – reduce them to a few ingratiating scars on my harelip?

6

By staving off the mysterious death of Architecture as we know it, I cheated myself of an empty contentedness. The suite was full of necessities. Tinting spansules is a profession, yes. Disconcerting, but true. But what about the statue in the hall outside? Who is this 'Horst'?

7

The authorities here are highly susp – shush! OK to take this down. Che is going into market research, more relevant than doctoring the poor. OK to take this down, they don't give a flying fuck. Every life saved broadens the base of the population pyramid that much more, until its substrata ... slimy and fetid but with more energy than the 'thin-out' line near top ... OK, take this down, friend. Roaches, tarantulas, roaches, tarantulas: in convoys of ten each they hurry along the traffic lane marked with day-glo dots, and down the starveling's throat. The Big Divvy according to the (transmission problems, friend, bear with me) – in the fields at low enough level to circumvent the inevitability of mechanization taking command (sorry, pal, different feeder channel for the nonce – erratum: nuns) in which case the population pyramid (bye, folks, time to go underground again) will be restructured into an obelisk, squeezing the hierarchy into a more nakedly vertical pattern that makes it impossible for them to reproduce themselves in sufficient numbers – less intermingling, less sloppy pecking-order in-fighting, more intra-bureau phoning, more non-destruct memos, more solitude at one's booth, to which one is assigned early in life, but this obelisk isn't practical yet (hi, back again, it's me) – pyramid has years to go as long as its base keeps widening (say) five per cent per annum – then its weight is sufficiently diffused to reduce the rate of sinkage to (say) ten per cent per annum, which gives us (say) oh, 2050 may be a bit hectic and the pyramid may have to be converted into a rectangle: sarcophagus, with the lid hooked from the inside to cut down on hanky-panky – (no need to take the rest down: message is over) – golf pro has yen for daughter, not flabby henna mama – only daughter and school chum – gov't censor demands X number pesetas leave in snatches throbbing, with the one girl tracing on the other girl's boob: Che – finger writing, invisible. Audience thinks it's 'AMOR' – except for politics buffs.

8

Regular paintings in front of the arch with the discreet black curtain. Most interesting, such a hard glare beating down on the lilies (Utrillo), with the ballerina electric mixer (Duchamp) floating over the Tudor bed and its inviting sateen spread, reflected in the mirror, and the pretty couple in the background, their bodies lightly touching, staring at the dawn from the balcony. They've been talking all night, you can tell, because they're Romeo and Juliet, and they have a great many lines to get through without any mistakes, and what with the tricks of authentic pronunciation, and the subjunctive tenses coming at them so fast –

9

Men working very high up, suspended in big wooden crates. Night shifts all over the city are finishing up the white high-rises before the next onslaught of boondockers arrives, getting in on the proverbial ground-floor.

10

Che is so trusting re 'truth and consequences'. He's too Western, he has dreams of walking with Nixon through the native villages, they go in one, and light up, just sit there – Nixon is converted! He brings the brass next time – they're converted! Big Ten Day Speech to the U.S. Must stop 'exploiting' etc. Impeached naturally. Chaos: villages: smoke rises from distant chimney. Bumblebees crawling around the empty Bumblebee Tuna Can.

11

Racial memory last night of a facial memory. Of an infinite number of taps (raindrops on leaf for months, months) that go into making a stone more cushion-like when one drapes one's back across it, forming an upside-down horse-shoe shape. I love that sacrifice face! Generally a stoop-shouldered – better stop here so as not to scare off *turismo*.

Bests,

President Bela Lugosi

12

Impossible to get those leaves to NYC in time to be effective. Also the dosage. We're working on it, but even so, packaging is the hang-up. It's all yellow with cougar urine stains, and there are brown spots on the dosage instructions, on crucial words, such as A.M. and orifice and ballyhoo. Must, repeat MUST trace them to source up-jungle. Or else the normals will flounder in a morass of mini-

Hot Dog ends up Hot Girl.

13

Zouave to mustachio gent in Paris *pissoir*:
  'Why are you carrying so many loaves?'
  'Er – I live in the country – '
  'Feed *this* – non-organic – '

14

Crazier mix here. Spooning by the ocean, barricaded against the African Experience. Ill-fitting composites: hot pants, snoods, cloches, pink curlers hanging from plastic sandwich wedges on charm bracelets. Lady in evening dress – fervent movie kiss, thrusts against escort. Her VW takes off. With a happy sigh, on the outside looking out, aware he must hammer at the outer edge of the outmost shell of the new exterior phase, the gringo, wearing an immaculate white shirt, finished his last joint, swallowed his last mild pep pill, and crossed the frontier.

15

At the stroke of six, the lost panorama struck up its song.

Zone B   another in Zone H   Zone B
virile life   mad colonel   virile life
no facilities   cycle   no facilities
                natural zonings
                    ABCDE
                    cicadas
                    ABCDE
                natural zonings
bobbing   a leaf-cutter ant   bobbing
dismantle   Futbol Night Club   dismantle
Zone X   another in Zone W   Zone X

falling feathers   red   falling feathers
no operas   glutted mongrel   no operas
abolish W   Nazi bare patch   abolish W
                watch out you
                watch out you
                    cicadas
                watch out you
                watch out you
lit up birds circling over meat markets
wing edges   no FBI no FBI   wing edges
cut off Amazon mezzo-soprano in mid-cad

puma eyed guys lean out windows Sundays
humming songs of lives lived real heavy
grass rustles from ungainly cranings of
                beaks and masks
                beaks and masks
                milky
            trees and vines
            trees and vines
grass rustles from ungainly cranings of
humming songs of lives lived real heavy
puma-eyed guys lean out windows Sundays

sanitary gobbet   sun   sanitary gobbet
wing edge: saw   sun   saw: wing edge
rubber bra   firecracker   rubber bra
            death candy
            death candy
            do it
            death candy
            death candy
giant awakes   nodding off   giant awakes
men shovel the nuts will buy putt-putts
baby girders   nodding off   baby girders

some sort gov't loudspeaker answer here
bad gas   not firecracker not   bad gas
some sort gov't loudspeaker answer here
                watch out you two
                do it   do it
                      watch out
                do it   do it
                watch out you two
change subject   change subject
humming bird   humming bird
out of reach   feast   out of reach

let's fuck he said   let's fuck he said
Mawarye and Woxha   Mawarye and Woxha
me too he said   we fuck   he said me too
                watch out you two
                do it   do it
                      watch out
                do it   do it
                watch out you two
the honeyfish inside her bit off a cock
lost your cock   lost your cock
I know   Woxha weeps   I know

river way up   river way up
standing in water the hoofs of the cows
rot away and piranha bite off the teats
                9:45   9:45
                banana and coffee
                    'Ada'
                banana and coffee
                9:45   9:45
river entered the city in Fifties or so
triangular baskets in warehouse shadows
rain disposal   rain disposal

she told us not to   she told us not to
picked up   turu seed   picked up
picked up Mawarye   Mawarye picked up
                push in   push in
                make new make new
                    just fine
                make new make new
                push in   push in
let's fuck he said   let's fuck he said
Mawarye and Woxha   Woxha and Mawarye
me too he said   we fuck   he said me too

```
peer at shit      white worms     peer at shit
palm hearts          sun          palm hearts
vague bites       light sleep     vague bites
                   lovebirds
                      bus
                    heh-heh
                      bus
                   lovebirds
sex program         dunno         sex program
three in a bed      dream         three in a bed
dream             Birthday!          dream
```

```
overcast again      'Ada'      overcast again
departure today     'Ada'      departure today
live for a moment and light up a: Torre
                   lentils
                    feast
                    feast
                   lentils
white heron stared at the pleasure boat
one Paris one N Y C one Belém one Chicago
one Sao Paulo one Zurich one El Capitan
        sloth on tree     sloth on tree
                 fish leap
                    rum
                    sun
                    ate
```

KENNETH KOCH

Sleeping with Women

Caruso: a voice.

Naples: sleeping with women.

Women: sleeping in the dark.

Voices: a music.

Pompeii: a ruin.

Pompeii: sleeping with women.

Men sleeping with women, women sleeping with women, sheep sleeping with women, everything sleeping with women.

The guard: asking you for a light.

Women: asleep.

Yourself: asleep.

Everything south of Naples: asleep and sleeping with them.

Sleeping with women: as in the poems of Pascoli.

Sleeping with women: as in the rain, as in the snow.

Sleeping with women: by starlight, as if we were angels, sleeping on the train,

On the starry foam, asleep and sleeping with them – sleeping with women.

Mediterranean: a voice.

Mediterranean: a sea. Asleep and sleeping.

Streetcar in Oslo, sleeping with women, Toonerville Trolley

In Stockholm asleep and sleeping with them, in Skansen

Alone, alone with women,

The rain sleeping with women, the brain of the dog-eyed genius

Alone, sleeping with women, all he has wanted,

The dog-eyed fearless man.

Sleeping with them: as in *The Perils of Pauline*

Asleep with them: as in Tosca
Sleeping with women and causing all that trouble
As in Roumania, as in Yugoslavia
Asleep and sleeping with them
Anti-Semitic, and sleeping with women,
Pro-canary, Rashomon, Shakespeare, tonight, sleeping
    with women
A big guy sleeping with women
A black seacoast's sleeve, asleep with them
And sleeping with women, and sleeping with them
The Greek islands sleeping with women
The muddy sky, asleep and sleeping with them.
Sleeping with women, as in a scholarly design
Sleeping with women, as if green polarity were a line
Into the sea, sleeping with women
As if wolverines, in a street line, as if sheep harbors
Could come alive from sleeping with women, wolverines
Greek islands sleeping with women, Nassos, Naxos, Kos,
Asleep with women, Mykonos, miotis,
And myositis, sleeping with women, blue-eyed
Red-eyed, green-eyed, yellow reputed, white-eyed women
Asleep and sleeping with them, blue, sleeping with women
As in love, as at sea, the rabbi, asleep and sleeping with
    them
As if that could be, the stones, the restaurant, asleep and
    sleeping with them,
Sleeping with women, as if they were knee
Arm and thigh asleep and sleeping with them, sleeping
    with women.
And the iris peg of the sea
Sleeping with women
And the diet pill of the tree
Sleeping with women
And the apology the goon the candlelight

The groan: asking you for the night, sleeping with women
Asleep and sleeping with them, the green tree
The iris, the swan: the building with its mouth open
Asleep with women, awake with man,
The sunlight, asleep and sleeping with them, the moving
    gong
The abacus, the crab, asleep and sleeping with them
And moving, and the moving van, in London, asleep with
    women
And intentions, inventions for sleeping with them
Lands sleeping with women, ants sleeping with women,
    Italo-Greek or Anglo-French orchestras
Asleep with women, asleep and sleeping with them,
The foam and the sleet, asleep and sleeping with them,
The schoolboy's poem, the crippled leg
Asleep and sleeping with them, sleeping with women
Sleeping with women, as if you were a purist
Asleep and sleeping with them.
Sleeping with women: there is no known form for the
    future
Of this undreamed-of view: sleeping with a chorus
Of highly tuned women, asleep and sleeping with them.
Bees, sleeping with women
And tourists, sleeping with them
Soap, sleeping with women; beds, sleeping with women
The universe: a choice
The headline: a voice, sleeping with women
At dawn, sleeping with women, asleep and sleeping with
    them.
Sleeping with women: a choice, as of a mule
As of an island, asleep or sleeping with them, as of a
    Russia,
As of an island, as of a drum: a choice of views: asleep and
    sleeping with them, as of high noon, as of a choice, as

of variety, as of the sunlight, red student, asleep and
    sleeping with them,
As with an orchid, as with an oriole, at school, sleeping
    with women, and you are the one
The one sleeping with women, in Mexico, sleeping with
    women
The ghost land, the vectors, sleeping with women
The motel man, the viaduct, the sun
The universe: a question
The moat: a cathexis
What have we done? On Rhodes, man
On Samos, dog
Sleeping with women
In the rain and in the sun
The dog has a red eye, it is November
Asleep and sleeping with them, sleeping with women
This June: a boy
October: sleeping with women
The motto: a sign; the bridge: a definition.
To the goat: destroy; to the rain: be a settee.
O rain of joy: sleeping with women, asleep and sleeping
    with them.
Volcano, Naples, Caruso, asleep and sleeping, asleep and
    sleeping with them
The window, the windrow, the hedgerow, irretrievable
    blue,
Sleeping with women, the haymow, asleep and sleeping
    with them, the canal
Asleep and sleeping with them, the eagle's feather, the
    dock's weather, and the glue:
Sleeping with you; asleep and sleeping with you: sleeping
    with women.
Sleeping with women, charming aspirin, as in the rain, as in
    the snow,

Asleep and sleeping with you: as if the crossbow, as of the
    moonlight
Sleeping with women: as if the tractate, as if d'Annunzio
Asleep and sleeping with you, asleep with women
Asleep and sleeping with you, asleep with women, asleep
    and sleeping with you, sleeping with women
As if the sun, as of Venice and the Middle Ages' 'true
Renaissance had just barely walked by the yucca
Forest' asleep and sleeping with you
In China, on parade, sleeping with women
And in the sun, asleep and sleeping with you, sleeping
    with women,
Asleep with women, the docks, the alley, and the prude
Sleeping with women, asleep with them.
The dune god: sleeping with women
The dove: asleep and sleeping with them
Dials sleeping with women; cybernetic tiles asleep and
    sleeping with them
Naples: sleeping with women; the short of breath
Asleep and sleeping with you, sleeping with women
As if I were you – moon idealism
Sleeping with women, pieces of stageboard, sleeping with
    women
The silent bus ride, sleeping with you.
The chore: sleeping with women
The force of a disaster: sleeping with you
The organ grinder's daughter: asleep with bitumen, sun-
    shine, sleeping with women,
Sleeping with women: in Greece, in China, in Italy, sleep-
    ing with blue
Red green orange and white women, sleeping with two
Three four and five women, sleeping on the outside
And on the inside of women, a violin, like a vista, women,
    sleeping with women

In the month of May, in June, in July
Sleeping with women, 'I watched my life go by' sleeping
    with women
A door of pine, a stormfilled valentine asleep and sleeping
    with them
'This Sunday heart of mine' profoundly dormoozed with
    them
They running and laughing, asleep and sleeping with
    them
'This idle heart of mine' insanely 'shlamoozed' asleep and
    sleeping with them,
They running in laughter
To the nearest time, oh doors of eternity
Oh young women's doors of my own time! sleeping with
    women
Asleep and sleeping with them, all Naples asleep and
    sleeping with them,
Venice sleeping with women, Burgos sleeping with
    women, Lausanne sleeping with women, hail depth-
    divers
Sleeping with women, and there is the bonfire of Crete
Catching divorce in its fingers, purple sleeping with
    women
And the red lights of dawn, have you ever seen them, green
    ports sleeping with women, acrobats and pawns,
You had not known it ere I told it you asleep with women
The Via Appia Antica asleep with women, asleep and sleep-
    ing with them
All beautiful objects, each ugly object, the intelligent world,
The arena of the spirits, the dietetic whisky, the storms
Sleeping with women, asleep and sleeping with them,
Sleeping with women. And the churches in Antigua,
    sleeping with women
The stone: a vow

The Nereid: a promise – to sleep with women
The cold – a convention: sleeping with women
The carriage: sleeping with women
The time: sometimes
The certainty: now
The soapbox: sleeping with women
The time and again nubile and time, sleeping with women,
    and the time now
Asleep and sleeping with them, asleep and asleep, sleeping
    with women, asleep and sleeping with them, sleeping
    with women.

In Love with You

I

O what a physical effect it has on me
To dive forever into the light blue sea
Of your acquaintance! Ah, but dearest friends,
Like forms, are finished, as life has ends! Still,
It is beautiful, when October
Is over, and February is over,
To sit in the starch of my shirt, and to dream of your sweet
Ways! As if the world were a taxi, you enter it, then
Reply (to no one), 'Let's go five or six blocks.'
Isn't the blue stream that runs past you a translation from
    the Russian?
Aren't my eyes bigger than love?
Isn't this history, and aren't we a couple of ruins?
Is Carthage Pompeii? is the pillow the bed? is the sun
What glues our heads together? O midnight! O midnight!
Is love what we are,
Or has happiness come to me in a private car
That's so very small I'm amazed to see it there?

2

We walk through the park in the sun, and you say, 'There's
    a spider
Of shadow touching the bench, when morning's begun.'
    I love you.
I love you fame I love you raining sun I love you cigarettes
    I love you love
I love you daggers I love smiles daggers and symbolism.

3

Inside the symposium of your sweetest look's

Sunflower awning by the nurse-faced chrysanthemums
childhood

Again represents a summer spent sticking knives into por-
celain raspberries, when China's

Still a country! Oh, King Edward abdicated years later,
that's

Exactly when. If you were seventy thousand years old,
and I were a pill,

I know I could cure your headache, like playing baseball
in drinking-water, as baskets

Of towels sweetly touch the bathroom floor! O benches of
nothing

Appear and reappear – electricity! I'd love to be how
You are, as if

The world were new, and the selves were blue

Which we don

When it's dawn,

Until evening puts on

The gray hooded selves and the light brown selves of . . .

Water! your tear-colored nail polish

Kisses me! and the lumberyard seems new

As a calm

On the sea, where, like pigeons,

I feel so mutated, sad, so breezed, so revivified, and still
so unabdicated –

Not like an edge of land coming over the sea!

The Circus

I

We will have to go away, said the girls in the circus
And never come back any more. There is not enough of an
audience
In this little town. Waiting against the black, blue sky
The big circus chariots took them into their entrances.
The light rang out over the hill where the circus wagons
dimmed away.
Underneath their dresses the circus girls were sweating,
But then, an orange tight sticking to her, one spoke with
Blue eyes, she was young and pretty, blonde
With bright eyes, and she spoke with her mouth open
when she sneezed
Lightly against the backs of the other girls waiting in line
To clock the rope, or come spinning down with her teeth
on the line,
And she said that the circus might leave – and red posters
Stuck to the outside of the wagon, it was beginning to
Rain – she said might leave but not her heart would ever
leave
Not that town but just any one where they had been,
risking their lives,
And that each place they were should be celebrated by
blue rosemary
In a patch, in the town. But they laughed and said Senti-
mental
Blonde, and she laughed, and they all, circus girls, clinging
To each other as the circus wagons rushed through the
night.

2

In the next wagon, the one forward of theirs, the next
    wagon
Was the elephants' wagon. A grey trunk dragged on the
    floor . . .

3

Orville the Midget tramped up and down. Paul the
    Separated Man
Leaped forward. It rained and rained. Some people in the
    cities
Where they passed through were sitting behind thick glass
Windows, talking about their brats and drinking chocolate
    syrup.

4

Minnie the Rabbit fingered her machine gun.
The bright day was golden.
She aimed the immense pine needle at the foxes
Thinking Now they will never hurt my tribe any more.

5

The circus wagons stopped during the night
For eighteen minutes in a little town called Rosebud,
    Nebraska.
It was after dinner it was after bedtime it was after nausea
    it was
After lunchroom. The girls came out and touched each
    other and had fun
And just had time to get a breath of the fresh air of the
    night in
Before the ungodly procession began once more down the
    purple highway.

6

With what pomp and ceremony the circus arrived orange
and red in the dawn!
It was exhausted, cars and wagons, and it lay down and
leaped
Forward a little bit, like a fox. Minnie the Rabbit shot a
little woolen bullet at it,
And just then the elephant man came to his doorway in the
sunlight and stood still.

7

The snoring circus master wakes up, he takes it on himself
to arrange the circus.
Soon the big tent floats high. Birds sing on the tent.
The parade girls and the living statue girls and the trapeze
girls
Cover their sweet young bodies with phosphorescent paint.
Some of the circus girls are older women, but each is
beautiful.
They stand, waiting for their cues, at the doorway of the
tent.
The sky-blue lion tamer comes in, and the red giraffe
manager.
They are very brave and wistful, and they look at the girls.
Some of the circus girls feel a hot sweet longing in their
bodies.
But now is it time for the elephants!
Slowly the giant beasts march in. Some of their legs are
clothed in blue papier-maché ruffles.
One has a red eye. The elephant man is at the peak of
happiness.
He speaks, giddily, to every one of the circus people he
passes,

He does not know what he is saying, he does not care –
His elephants are on display! They walk into the sandy
  ring . . .

8

Suddenly a great scream breaks out in the circus tent!
It is Aileen the trapeze artist, she has fallen into the dust
  and dirt
From so high! She must be dead! The stretcher bearers
  rush out,
They see her lovely human form clothed in red and white
  and orange wiry net,
And they see that she does not breathe any more.
The circus doctor leaves his tent, he runs out to care for
  Aileen.
He traverses the circus grounds and the dusty floor of the
  circus entrance, and he comes
Where she is, now she has begun to move again, she is not
  dead,
But the doctor tells her he does not know if she will ever
  be able to perform on the trapeze again,
And he sees the beautiful orange and red and white form
  shaken with sobs,
And he puts his hand on her forehead and tells her she must
  lie still.

9

The circus girls form a cortege, they stand in file in the
  yellow and white sunlight.
'What is death in the circus? That depends on if it is spring.
Then, if elephants are there, *mon père*, we are not completely
  lost.
Oh the sweet strong odor of beasts which laughs at decay!

Decay! decay! We are like the elements in a kaleidoscope,
But such passions we feel! bigger than beaches and
Rustier than harpoons.' After his speech the circus prac-
 titioner sat down.

10

Minnie the Rabbit felt the blood leaving her little body
As she lay in the snow, orange and red and white,
A beautiful design. The dog laughs, his tongue hangs out,
 he looks at the sky.
It is white. The master comes. He laughs. He picks up
 Minnie the Rabbit
And ties her to a pine tree bough, and leaves.

11

Soon through the forest came the impassioned bumble bee.
He saw the white form on the bough. 'Like rosebuds
 when you are thirteen,' said Elmer.
Iris noticed that he didn't have any cap on.
'You must be polite when mother comes,' she said.
The sky began to get grey, then the snow came.
The two tots pressed together. Elmer opened his mouth
 and let the snow fall in it. Iris felt warm and happy.

12

Bang! went the flyswatter. Mr Watkins, the circus manager,
 looked around the room.
'Damn it, damn these flies!' he said. Mr Loftus, the circus
 clerk, stared at the fly interior he had just exposed.

The circus doctor stood beside the lake. In his hand he had
 a black briefcase.
A wind ruffled the surface of the lake and slightly rocked the
 boats.

Red and green fish swam beneath the surface of the water.
The doctor went into the lunchroom and sat down. No,
    he said, he didn't care for anything to eat.
The soft wind of summer blew in the light green trees.

The Artist

Ah, well, I abandon you, cherrywood smokestack,
Near the entrance to this old green park! ...

*   *   *

Cherrywood avalanche, my statue of you
Is still standing in Toledo, Ohio.
O places, summer, boredom, the static of an acrobatic blue!

And I made an amazing zinc airliner
It is standing to this day in the Minneapolis zoo ...

Old times are not so long ago, plaster-of-paris haircut!

*   *   *

I often think *Play* was my best work.
It is an open field with a few boards in it.

Children are allowed to come and play in *Play*
By permission of the Cleveland Museum.
I look up at the white clouds, I wonder what I shall do,
    and smile.

Perhaps somebody will grow up having been influenced
    by *Play*,
I think – but what good will that do?
Meanwhile I am interested in steel cigarettes ...

*   *   *

The orders are coming in thick and fast for steel cigarettes,
    steel cigars.
The Indianapolis Museum has requested six dozen
    packages.

I wonder if I'd still have the courage to do a thing like
    Play?

I think I may go to Cleveland . . .

            *   *   *

Well, here I am! Pardon me, can you tell me how to get to
    the Cleveland Museum's monumental area, *Play*?
'Mister, that was torn down a long time ago. You ought
    to go and see the new thing they have now – *Gun.*'
What? *Play* torn down?
'Yes, Mister, and I loved to climb in it too, when I was a
    kid!' And he shakes his head
Sadly . . . But I am thrilled beyond expectation!
He liked my work!
And I guess there must be others like that man in Cleveland
    too . . .

So you see, *Play* has really had its effect!
Now I am on the outskirts of town
And . . . here it is! But it has changed! There are some blue
    merds lying in the field
And it's not marked *Play* anymore – and here's a calf!
I'm so happy, I can't tell why!
Was this how I originally imagined *Play*, but lacked the
    courage?

It would be hard now, though, to sell it to another museum.
I wonder if the man I met's children will come and play in
    it?
How does one's audience survive?

            *   *   *

Pittsburgh, May 16th. I have abandoned the steel cigarettes.
I am working on *Bee*.
Bee will be a sixty-yards-long covering for the elevator
shaft opening in the foundry sub-basement
Near my home. So far it's white sailcloth with streams of
golden paint evenly spaced out
With a small blue pond at one end, and around it orange
and green flowers. My experience in Cleveland affected
me so
That my throat aches whenever I am not working at full
speed. I have never been so happy and inspired and
Play seems to me now like a juvenile experience!

*   *   *

June 8th. *Bee* is still not finished. I have introduced a huge
number of red balloons into it. How will it work?
Yesterday X. said, 'Are you still working on *Bee*? What's
happened to your interest in steel cigarettes?'
Y. said, 'He hasn't been doing any work at all on them
since he went to Cleveland.' A shrewd guess! But how
much can they possibly know?

*   *   *

November 19th. Disaster! *Bee* was almost completed, and
now the immense central piece of sailcloth has torn.
Impossible to repair it!

December 4th. I've gone back to work on *Bee*! I suddenly
thought (after weeks of despair!), 'I can place the balloons
over the tear in the canvas!' So that is what I am doing.
All promises to be well!

December 6th. The foreman of the foundry wants to look
at my work. It seems that he too is an 'artist' – does

sketches and watercolors and such ... What will he
think of *Bee*?

* * *

Cherrywood! I had left you far from my home
And the foreman came to look at *Bee*
And the zinc airliner flew into *Play*!

The pink balloons aren't heavy, but the yellow ones break.
The foreman says, 'It's the greatest thing I ever saw!'
Cleveland heard too and wants me to come back and
reinaugurate *Play*

I dream of going to Cleveland but never will
Bee has obsessed my mind.

* * *

March 14th. A cold spring day. It is snowing. *Bee* is completed.

* * *

O *Bee* I think you are my best work
In the blue snow-filled air
I feel my heart break
I lie down in the snow
They come from the foundry and take *Bee* away
Oh what can I create now, Earth,

Green Earth on which everything blossoms anew?
'A bathroom floor cardboard trolley line
The shape and size of a lemon seed with on the inside
A passenger the size of a pomegranate seed
Who is an invalid and has to lean on the cardboard side

Of the lemon-seed-sized trolley line so that he won't fall
off the train.'

*   *   *

*   *   *

I just found these notes written many years ago.
How seriously I always take myself! Let it be a lesson to
me.
To bring things up to date: I have just finished *Campaign*,
which is a tremendous piece of charcoal.
Its shape is difficult to describe; but it is extremely large
and would reach to the sixth floor of the Empire State
Building. I have been very successful in the past fourteen
or fifteen years.

*   *   *

Summer Night, shall I never succeed in finishing you? Oh
you are the absolute end of all my creation! The ethereal
beauty of that practically infinite number of white stone
slabs stretching into the blue secrecy of ink! O stabs in
my heart!

. . . Why not a work *Stabs in My Heart*? But *Summer Night*?

January . . . A troubled sleep. Can I make two things at
once? What way is there to be sure that the impulse to
work on *Stabs in My Heart* is serious? It seems occasioned
only by my problem about finishing *Summer Night* . . . ?

*   *   *

The *Magician of Cincinnati* is now ready for human use.
They are twenty-five tremendous stone staircases, each
over six hundred feet high, which will be placed in the

Ohio River between Cincinnati and Louisville, Kentucky. All the boats coming down the Ohio River will presumably be smashed up against the immense statues, which are the most recent work of the creator of *Flowers*, *Bee*, *Play*, *Again* and *Human Use*. Five thousand citizens are thronged on the banks of the Ohio waiting to see the installation of the work, and the crowd is expected to be more than fifteen times its present number before morning. There will be a game of water baseball in the early afternoon, before the beginning of the ceremonies, between the Cincinnati Redlegs and the Pittsburgh Pirates. The *Magician of Cincinnati*, incidentally, is said to be absolutely impregnable to destruction of any kind, and will therefore presumably always be a feature of this part of the Ohio . . .

*   *   *

May 16th. With what an intense joy I watched the installation of the *Magician of Cincinnati* today, in the Ohio River, where it belongs, and which is so much a part of my original scheme . . .

May 17th. I feel suddenly freed from life – not so much as if my work were going to change, but as though I had at last seen what I had so long been prevented (perhaps I prevented myself!) from seeing: that there is too much for me to do. Somehow this enables me to relax, to breathe easily . . .

*   *   *

There's the *Magician of Cincinnati*
In the distance
Here I am in the green trees of Pennsylvania

How strange I felt when they had installed
The *Magician*! ... Now a bluebird trills, I am busy making
   my polished stones
For *Dresser*.

The stream the stone the birds the reddish-pink Penn-
   sylvania hills
All go to make up *Dresser*
Why am I camping out?
I am waiting for the thousands of tons of embalming fluid
That have to come and with which I can make these hills.

*   *   *

GREATEST ARTISTIC EVENT HINTED BY GOVERNOR

Reading, June 4. Greatest artistic event was hinted today
   by governor. Animals converge on meadow where artist
   working.

CONVERGE ON MEADOW WHERE WORK-ING

ARTIST HINTED, SAME MAN

... the *Magician of Cincinnati*

THREE YEARS

October 14th. I want these hills to be striated! How naive
   the *Magician of Cincinnati* was! Though it makes me
   happy to think of it ... Here, I am plunged into such
   real earth! Striate, hills! What is this deer's head of green
   stone? I can't fabricate anything less than what I think
   should girdle the earth ...

KENNETH KOCH

PHOTOGRAPH

PHOTOGRAPH

PHOTOGRAPH

Artist who created the *Magician of Cincinnati*; Now at work in Pennsylvania; The Project – *Dresser* – So Far.

* * *

Ah! ...

* * *

TONS

SILICON, GRASS AND DEER-HEAD RANGE
Philadelphia. Your voice as well as mine will be appreciated to express the appreciation of *Dresser*, which makes of Pennsylvania the silicon, grass and stone deer-head center of the world ... Artist says he may change his mind about the central bridges. Fountains to give forth real tar-water. Mountain lake in center. Real chalk cliffs. Also cliffs of clay. Deep declivities nearby. 'Wanted forest atmosphere, yet to be open.' Gas ...

* * *

PHOTOGRAPH

SKETCH

DEDICATION CEREMONY

GOES SWIMMING IN OWN STREAM

SHAKING HANDS WITH GOVERNOR

COLOR PICTURE

THE HEAD OF THE ARTIST

THE ARTIST'S HAND

STACK OF ACTUAL BILLS NEEDED TO PAY
   FOR PROJECT

Story of *Dresser*

PENNSYLVANIA'S PRIDE: *DRESSER*

Creator of *Dresser*

*   *   *

STILL SMILING AT FORGE
Beverly, South Dakota, April 18. Still smiling at forge,
artist of *Dresser* says, 'No, of course I haven't forgotten
Dresser. Though how quickly the years have gone by
since I have been doing *Too!*' We glanced up at the sky
and saw a large white bird, somewhat similar to an
immense seagull, which was as if fixed above our heads.
Its eyes were blue sapphires, and its wings were formed
by an ingenious arrangement of whitened daffodil-
blossom parts. Its body seemed mainly charcoal, on the
whole, with a good deal of sand mixed in. As we watched
it, the creature actually seemed to move . . .

August 4th . . . Three four five, and it's finished! I can see
   it in Beverly . . .

*   *   *

BEVERLY   HONORS   ARTIST.   CALLED
'FOUNDING FATHER'

KENNETH KOCH

Beverly, South Dakota, August 14 ...

MISSISSIPPI CLAIMS BIRTHPLACE

HONORS BIRTHPLACE

BIRTHPLACE HONORS HELD

* * *

INDIANS AND SAVANTS MEET TO PRAISE
  WEST WIND

PAT HONORED

PAT AND *WEST WIND* HONORED

* * *

June 3rd. It doesn't seem possible – the Pacific Ocean! I
  have ordered sixteen million tons of blue paint. Waiting
  anxiously for it to arrive. How would grass be as a
  substitute? cement?

* * *

1955

Fresh Air

I

At the Poem Society a black-haired man stands up to say
'You make me sick with all your talk about restraint and
mature talent!
Haven't you ever looked out the window at a painting by
Matisse,
Or did you always stay in hotels where there were too
many spiders crawling on your visages?
Did you ever glance inside a bottle of sparkling pop,
Or see a citizen split in two by the lightning?
I am afraid you have never smiled at the hibernation
Of bear cubs except that you saw in it some deep relation
To human suffering and wishes, oh what a bunch of
crackpots!'
The black-haired man sits down, and the others shoot
arrows at him.
A blond man stands up and says,
'He is right! Why should we be organized to defend the
kingdom
Of dullness? There are so many slimy people connected
with poetry,
Too, and people who know nothing about it!
I am not recommending that poets like each other and
organize to fight them,
But simply that lightning should strike them.'
Then the assembled mediocrities shot arrows at the blond-
haired man.
The chairman stood up on the platform, oh he was physi-
cally ugly!
He was small-limbed and -boned and thought he was quite
seductive,

But he was bald with certain hideous black hairs,

And his voice had the sound of water leaving a vaseline
bathtub,

And he said, 'The subject for this evening's discussion is
poetry

On the subject of love between swans.' And everyone threw
candy hearts

At the disgusting man, and they stuck to his bib and tucker,

And he danced up and down on the platform in terrific
glee

And recited the poetry of his little friends – but the blond
man stuck his head

Out of a cloud and recited poems about the east and
thunder,

And the black-haired man moved through the stratosphere
chanting

Poems of the relationships between terrific prehistoric
charcoal whales,

And the slimy man with candy hearts sticking all over him

Wilted away like a cigarette paper on which the bumblebees
have urinated,

And all the professors left the room to go back to their duty,

And all that were left in the room were five or six poets

And together they sang the new poem of the twentieth
century

Which, though influenced by Mallarmé, Shelley, Byron,
and Whitman,

Plus a million other poets, is still entirely original

And is so exciting that it cannot be here repeated.

You must go to the Poem Society and wait for it to happen.

Once you have heard this poem you will not love any
other,

Once you have dreamed this dream you will be inconsol-
able,

Once you have loved this dream you will be as one dead,
Once you have visited the passages of this time's great art!

2

'Oh to be seventeen years old
Once again,' sang the red-haired man, 'and not know that
  poetry
Is ruled with the sceptre of the dumb, the deaf, and the
  creepy!'
And the shouting persons battered his immortal body with
  stones
And threw his primitive comedy into the sea
From which it sang forth poems irrevocably blue.

Who are the great poets of our time, and what are their
  names?
Yeats of the baleful influence, Auden of the baleful in-
  fluence, Eliot of the baleful influence
(Is Eliot a great poet? no one knows), Hardy, Stevens,
  Williams (is Hardy of our time?),
Hopkins (is Hopkins of our time?), Rilke (is Rilke of our
  time?), Lorca (is Lorca of our time?), who is still of our
  time?
Mallarmé, Valéry, Apollinaire, Eluard, Reverdy, French
  poets are still of our time,
Pasternak and Mayakovsky, is Jouve of our time?

Where are young poets in America, they are trembling in
  publishing houses and universities,
Above all they are trembling in universities, they are bath-
  ing the library steps with their spit,
They are gargling out innocuous (to whom?) poems about
  maple trees and their children,

Sometimes they brave a subject like the Villa d'Este or a
    lighthouse in Rhode Island,
Oh what worms they are! they wish to perfect their form.
Yet could not these young men, put in another profession,
Succeed admirably, say at sailing a ship? I do not doubt
    it, Sir, and I wish we could try them.
(A plane flies over the ship holding a bomb but perhaps it
    will not drop the bomb,
The young poets from the universities are staring anxiously
    at the skies,
Oh they are remembering their days on the campus when
    they looked up to watch birds excrete,
They are remembering the days they spent making their
    elegant poems.)

Is there no voice to cry out from the wind and say what it is
    like to be the wind,
To be roughed up by the trees and to bring music from the
    scattered houses
And the stones, and to be in such intimate relationship with
    the sea
That you cannot understand it? Is there no one who feels
    like a pair of pants?

3

Summer in the trees! 'It is time to strangle several bad
    poets.'
The yellow hobbyhorse rocks to and fro, and from the
    chimney
Drops the Strangler! The white and pink roses are slightly
    agitated by the struggle,
But afterwards beside the dead 'poet' they cuddle up
    comfortingly against their vase. They are safer now, no
    one will compare them to the sea.

Here on the railroad train, one more time, is the Strangler.
He is going to get that one there, who is on his way to a
poetry reading.
Agh! Biff! A body falls to the moving floor.

In the football stadium I also see him,
He leaps through the frosty air at the maker of com-
parisons
Between football and life and silently, silently strangles
him!

Here is the Strangler dressed in a cowboy suit
Leaping from his horse to annihilate the students of myth!

The Strangler's ear is alert for the names of Orpheus,
Cuchulain, Gawain, and Odysseus,
And for poems addressed to Jane Austen, F. Scott Fitz-
gerald,
To Ezra Pound, and to personages no longer living
Even in anyone's thoughts – O Strangler the Strangler!

He lies on his back in the waves of the Pacific Ocean.

4

Supposing that one walks out into the air
On a fresh spring day and has the misfortune
To encounter an article on modern poetry
In *New World Writing*, or has the misfortune
To see some examples of some of the poetry
Written by the men with their eyes on the myth
And the Missus and the midterms, in the *Hudson Review*;
Or, if one is abroad, in *Botteghe Oscure*,
Or indeed in *Encounter*, what is one to do
With the rest of one's day that lies blasted to ruins

All bluely about one, what is one to do?
O surely one cannot complain to the President,
Nor even to the deans of Columbia College,
Nor to T. S. Eliot, nor to Ezra Pound,
And supposing one writes to the Princess Caetani,
'Your poets are awful!' what good would it do?
And supposing one goes to the *Hudson Review*
With a package of matches and sets fire to the building?
One ends up in prison with trial subscriptions
To the *Partisan, Sewanee,* and *Kenyon Review*!

5

Sun out! perhaps there is a reason for the lack of poetry
In these ill-contented souls, perhaps they need air!

Blue air, fresh air, come in, I welcome you, you are an art
    student,
Take off your cap and gown and sit down on the chair.
Together we shall paint the poets – but no, air! perhaps you
    should go to them, quickly,
Give them a little inspiration, they need it, perhaps they
    are out of breath,
Give them a little inhuman company before they freeze the
    English language to death!
(And rust their typewriters a little, be sea air! be noxious!
    kill them, if you must, but stop their poetry!
I remember I saw you dancing on the surf on the Côte
    d'Azur,
And I stopped, taking my hat off, but you did not remember
    me,
Then afterwards you came to my room bearing a handful
    of orange flowers
And we were together all through the summer night!)

That we might go away together, it is so beautiful on the
   sea, there are a few white clouds in the sky!

But no, air! you must go ... Ah, stay!

But she has departed and ... Ugh! what poisonous fumes
   and clouds! what a suffocating atmosphere!
Cough! whose are these hideous faces I see, what is this
   rigor
Infecting the mind? where are the green Azores,
Fond memories of childhood, and the pleasant orange
   trolleys,
A girl's face, red-white, and her breasts and calves, blue
   eyes, brown eyes, green eyes, fahrenheit
Temperatures, dandelions, and trains, O blue?!
Wind, wind, what is happening? Wind! I can't see any
   bird but the gull, and I feel it should symbolize ...
Oh, pardon me, there's a swan, one two three swans,
   a great white swan, hahaha how pretty they are!
   Smack!
Oh! stop! help! yes, I see – disrespect of my superiors –
   forgive me, dear Zeus, nice Zeus, parabolic bird, O
   feathered excellence! white!
There is Achilles too, and there's Ulysses, I've always
   wanted to see them, hahaha!
And there is Helen of Troy, I suppose she is Zeus too, she's
   so terribly pretty – hello, Zeus, my you are beautiful,
   Bang!
One more mistake and I get thrown out of the Modern
   Poetry Association, help! Why aren't there any adjec-
   tives around?
Oh there are, there's practically nothing else – look, here's
   *grey, utter, agonized, total, phenomenal, gracile, invidious,
   sundered,* and *fused,*

Elegant, absolute, pyramidal, and ... Scream! but what can I
describe with these words? States!

States symbolized and divided by two, complex states,
magic states, states of consciousness governed by an
aroused sincerity, cockadoodle doo!

Another bird! is it morning? Help! where am I? am I in
the barnyard? oink oink, scratch, moo! Splash!

My first lesson. 'Look around you. What do you think and
feel?' *Uhhh* ... 'Quickly!' *This Connecticut landscape would
have pleased Vermeer.* Wham! A-Plus. 'Congratulations!'
I am promoted.

OOOhhhhh I wish I were dead, what a headache! My
second lesson: 'Rewrite your first lesson line six hundred
times. Try to make it into a magnetic field.' I can do it
too. But my poor line! What a nightmare! Here comes
a tremendous horse,

Trojan, I presume. No, it's my third lesson. 'Look, look!
Watch him, see what he's doing? That's what we want
you to do. Of course it won't be the same as his at first,
but ...' I demur. Is there no other way to fertilize
minds?

Bang! I give in ... Already I see my name in two or three
anthologies, a serving girl comes into the barn bringing
me the anthologies,

She is very pretty and I smile at her a little sadly, perhaps
it is my last smile! Perhaps she will hit me! But no, she
smiles in return, and she takes my hand.

My hand, my hand! what is this strange thing I feel in
my hand, on my arm, on my chest, my face – can it
be ... ? it is! AIR!

Air, air, you've come back! Did you have any success?
'What do you think?' I don't know, air. You are so
strong, air.

And she breaks my chains of straw, and we walk down the
    road, behind us the hideous fumes!
Soon we reach the seaside, she is a young art student who
    places her head on my shoulder,
I kiss her warm red lips, and here is the Strangler, reading
    the *Kenyon Review*! Good luck to you, Strangler!
Goodbye, Helen! goodbye, fumes! goodbye, abstracted
    dried-up boys! goodbye, dead trees! goodbye, skunks!
Goodbye, manure! goodbye, critical manicure! goodbye,
    you big fat men standing on the east coast as well as the
    west giving poems the test! farewell, Valéry's stern dic-
    tum!
Until tomorrow, then, scum floating on the surface of
    poetry! goodbye for a moment, refuse that happens to
    land in poetry's boundaries! adieu, stale eggs teaching
    imbeciles poetry to bolster up your egos! adios, boring
    anomalies of these same stale eggs!
Ah, but the scum is deep! Come, let me help you! and soon
    we pass into the clear blue water. Oh GOODBYE,
    castrati of poetry! farewell, stale pale skunky pentameters
    (the only honest English meter, gloop gloop!) until
    tomorrow, horrors! oh, farewell!

Hello, sea! good morning, sea! hello, clarity and excite-
    ment, you great expanse of green –

O green, beneath which all of them shall drown!

1955

Permanently

One day the Nouns were clustered in the street.
An Adjective walked by, with her dark beauty.
The Nouns were struck, moved, changed.
The next day a Verb drove up, and created the Sentence.

Each Sentence says one thing – for example, 'Although
   it was a dark rainy day when the Adjective walked by,
   I shall remember the pure and sweet expression on her
   face until the day I perish from the green, effective
   earth.'
Or, 'Will you please close the window, Andrew?'
Or, for example, 'Thank you, the pink pot of flowers on
   the window sill has changed color recently to a light
   yellow, due to the heat from the boiler factory which
   exists nearby.'

In the springtime the Sentences and the Nouns lay silently
   on the grass.
A lonely Conjunction here and there would call, 'And!
   But!'
But the Adjective did not emerge.

As the adjective is lost in the sentence,
So I am lost in your eyes, ears, nose, and throat –
You have enchanted me with a single kiss
Which can never be undone
Until the destruction of language.

You Were Wearing

You were wearing your Edgar Allan Poe printed cotton
blouse.

In each divided up square of the blouse was a picture of
Edgar Allan Poe.

Your hair was blonde and you were cute. You asked me,
'Do most boys think that most girls are bad?'

I smelled the mould of your seaside resort hotel bedroom
on your hair held in place by a John Greenleaf Whittier
clip.

'No,' I said, 'it's girls who think that boys are bad.' Then
we read *Snowbound* together

And ran around in an attic, so that a little of the blue enamel
was scraped off my George Washington, Father of His
Country, shoes.

Mother was walking in the living room, her Strauss
Waltzes comb in her hair.

We waited for a time and then joined her, only to be served
tea in cups painted with pictures of Herman Melville

As well as with illustrations from his book *Moby Dick* and
from his novella, *Benito Cereno*.

Father came in wearing his Dick Tracy necktie: 'How about
a drink, everyone?'

I said, 'Let's go outside a while.' Then we went onto the
porch and sat on the Abraham Lincoln swing.

You sat on the eyes, mouth, and beard part, and I sat on
the knees.

In the yard across the street we saw a snowman holding a
garbage can lid smashed into a likeness of the mad
English king, George the Third.

Thank You

Oh thank you for giving me the chance
Of being ship's doctor! I am sorry that I shall have to
    refuse –
But, you see, the most I know of medicine is orange
    flowers
Tilted in the evening light against a cashmere red
Inside which breasts invent the laws of light
And of night, where cashmere moors itself across the sea.
And thank you for giving me these quintuplets
To rear and make happy ... My mind was on something
    else.

Thank you for giving me this battleship to wash,
But I have a rash on my hands and my eyes hurt,
And I know so little about cleaning a ship
That I should rather clean an island.
There one knows what one is about – sponge those palm
    trees, sweep up the sand a little, polish those coconuts;
Then take a rest for a while and it's time to trim the grass
    as well as separate it from each other where gummy
    substances have made individual blades stick together,
    forming an ugly bunch;
And then take the dead bark off the trees, and perfume
    these islands a bit with a song ... That's easy – but a
    battleship!
Where does one begin and how does one do? to batten
    the hatches? I would rather clean a million palm trees.

Now here comes an offer of a job for setting up a levee
In Mississippi. No thanks. Here it says *Rape or Worse*. I
    think they must want me to publicize this book.

On the jacket it says 'Published in Boothbay Harbor,
    Maine' – what a funny place to publish a book!
I suppose it is some provincial publishing house
Whose provincial pages emit the odor of sails
And the freshness of the sea
Breeze ... But publicity!
The only thing I could publicize well would be my tooth,
Which I could say came with my mouth and in a most
    engaging manner
With my whole self, my body and including my mind,
Spirits, emotions, spiritual essences, emotional substances,
    poetry, dreams, and lords
Of my life, everything, all embraceleted with my tooth
In a way that makes one wish to open the windows and
    scream 'Hi!' to the heavens,
And 'Oh, come and take me away before I die in a minute!'

It is possible that the dentist is smiling, that he dreams of
    extraction
Because he believes that the physical tooth and the spiritual
    tooth are one.

Here is another letter, this one from a textbook advertiser;
He wants me to advertise a book on chopping down trees.
But how could I? I love trees! and I haven't the slightest
    sympathy with chopping them down, even though I
    know
We need their products for wood-fires, some houses, and
    maple syrup –
Still I like trees better
In their standing condition, when they sway at the begin-
    ning of evening ...
And thank you for the pile of driftwood.
Am I wanted at the sea?

And thank you for the chance to run a small hotel
In an elephant stopover in Zambezi,
But I do not know how to take care of guests, certainly
    they would all leave soon
After seeing blue lights out the windows and rust on their
    iron beds – I'd rather own a bird-house in Jamaica:
Those people come in, the birds, they do not care how
    things are kept up . . .
It's true that Zambezi proprietorship would be exciting,
    with people getting off elephants and coming into my
    hotel,
But as tempting as it is I cannot agree.
And thank you for this offer of the post of referee
For the Danish wrestling championship – I simply do not
    feel qualified . . .
But the fresh spring air has been swabbing my mental
    decks
Until, although prepared for fight, still I sleep on land.
Thank you for the ostriches. I have not yet had time to
    pluck them,
But I am sure they will be delicious, adorning my plate at
    sunset,
My tremendous plate, and the plate
Of the offers to all my days. But I cannot fasten my exhilara-
    tion to the sun.

And thank you for the evening of the night on which I
    fell off my horse in the shadows. That was really useful.

Lunch

The lanternslides grinding out B-flat minor
Chords to the ears of the deaf youngster who sprays in
　　Hicksville
The sides of a car with the dream-splitting paint
Of pianos (he dreamt of one day cutting the Conservatory
In two with his talent), these lanternslides, I say,
They are – The old woman hesitated. A lifesaver was
　　shoved down her throat; then she continued:
They are some very good lanternslides in that bunch. Then
　　she fainted
And we revived her with flowers. She smiled sleepily at
　　the sun.
He is my own boy, she said, with her glass hand falling
　　through the sparkling red America of lunch.

That old boilermaker she has in her back yard,
Olaf said, used to be her sweetheart years back.
One day, though a train passed, and pressed her hard,
And she deserted life and love for liberty.
We carried Olaf softly into the back yard
And laid him down with his head under the steamroller.
Then Jill took the wheel and I tinkered with the engine,
Till we rolled him under, rolled him under the earth.
When people ask us what's in our back yard
Now, we don't like to tell them, Jill says, laying her silver
　　bandannaed head on my greened bronze shoulder.
Then we both dazzle ourselves with the red whiteness of
　　lunch.

That old woman named Tessie Runn
Had a tramp boyfriend who toasted a bun.
They went to Florida, but Maxine Schweitzer was hard of

Hearing and the day afterwards the judge adjourned the
    trial.
When it finally came for judgment to come up
Of delicious courtyards near the Pantheon,
At last we had to let them speak, the children whom flowers
    had made statues
For the rivers of water which came from their funnel;
And we stood there in the middle of existence
Dazzled by the white paraffin of lunch.

Music in Paris and water coming out from the flannel
Of the purist person galloping down the Madeleine
Toward a certain wafer. Hey! just a minute! the sunlight is
    being rifled
By the green architecture of the flowers. But the boulevard
    turned a big blue deaf ear
Of cinema placards to the detonated traveler. He had
    forgotten the blue defilade of lunch!

Genoa! a stone's throw from Acapulco
If an engine were built strong enough,
And down where the hulls and scungilli,
Glisteningly unconscious, agree,
I throw a game of shoes with Horace Sturnbul
And forget to eat lunch.

O launch, lunch, you dazzling hoary tunnel
To paradise!
Do you see that snowman tackled over there
By summer and the sea? A boardwalk went to Istanbul
And back under his left eye. We saw the Moslems praying
In Rhodes. One had a red fez, another had a black cap.
And in the extended heat of afternoon,
As an ice-cold gradual sweat covered my whole body,

I realized, and the carpet swam like a red world at my feet
In which nothing was green, and the Moslems went on
    praying,
That we had missed lunch, and a perpetual torrent roared
    into the sea
Of my understanding. An old woman gave us bread and
    rolls on the street.

The dancing wagon has come! here is the dancing wagon!
Come up and get lessons – here is lemonade and grammar!
Here is drugstore and cowboy – all that is America – plus
    sex, perfumes, and shimmers – all the Old World;
Come and get it – and here is your reading matter
For twenty-nine centuries, and here finally is lunch –
To be served in the green defilade under the roaring tower
Where Portugal meets Spain inside a flowered madeleine.

My ginger dress has nothing on, but yours
Has on a picture of Queen Anne Boleyn
Surrounded by her courtiers eating lunch
And on the back a one of Henry the Eighth
Summoning all his courtiers in for lunch.

And the lunchboat has arrived
From Spain.
Everyone getting sick is on it;
The bold people and the sadists are on it;
I am glad I am not on it,
I am having a big claw of garlic for lunch –
But it plucks me up in the air,
And there, above the ship, on a cloud
I see the angels eating lunch.
One has a beard, another a moustache,
And one has some mustard smeared on his ears.

A couple of them ask me if I want to go to Honolulu,
And I accept – it's all right –
Another time zone: we'll be able to have lunch.
They are very beautiful and transparent,
My two traveling companions,
And they will go very well with Hawaii
I realize as we land there,
That dazzling red whiteness – it is our desire . . .
For whom? The angels of lunch.

Oh I sat over a glass of red wine
And you came out dressed in a paper cup.
An ant-fly was eating hay-mire in the chair-rafters
And large white birds flew in and dropped edible animals
    to the ground.
If they had been gulls it would have been garbage
Or fish. We have to be fair to the animal kingdom,
But if I do not wish to be fair, if I wish to eat lunch
Undisturbed – ? The light of day shines down. The world
    continues.

We stood in the little hutment in Biarritz
Waiting for lunch, and your hand clasped mine
And I felt it was sweaty;
And then lunch was served,
Like the bouquet of an enchantress.
Oh the green whites and red yellows
And purple whites of lunch!

The bachelor eats his lunch,
The married man eats his lunch,
And old Uncle Joris belches
The seascape in which a child appears
Eating a watermelon and holding a straw hat.

He moves his lips as if to speak
But only sea air emanates from this childish beak.
It is the moment of sorrows,
And in the shores of history,
Which stretch in both directions, there are no happy
    tomorrows.
But Uncle Joris holds his apple up and begins to speak
To the child. Red waves fan my universe with the green
    macaw of lunch.

This street is deserted;
I think my eyes are empty;
Let us leave
Quickly.
Day bangs on the door and is gone.

Then they picked him up and carried him away from that
    company.
When he awoke he was in the fire department, and sleepy
    but not tired.
They gave him a hoseful of blue Spain to eat for lunch,
And Portugal was waiting for him at the door, like a rain-
    storm of evening raspberries.

It is time to give lunch to my throat and not my chest.
What? either the sting ray has eaten my lunch
Or else – and she searches the sky for something else;
But I am far away, seeming blue-eyed, empirical . . .
Let us give lunch to the lunch –
But how shall we do it?
The headwaiters expand and confer;
Will little pieces of cardboard box do it?
And what about silver and gold pellets?
The headwaiters expand and confer:

And what if the lunch should refuse to eat anything at all?
Why then we'd say be damned to it,
And the red doorway would open on a green railway
And the lunch would be put in a blue car
And it would go away to Whippoorwill Valley
Where it would meet and marry Samuel Dogfoot, and
    bring forth seven offspring,
All of whom would be half human, half lunch;
And when we saw them, sometimes, in the gloaming,
We would take off our mining hats and whistle Tweet
    twee-oo,
With watering mouths staring at the girls in pink organdy
    frocks,
Not realizing they really were half edible,
And we would die still without knowing it;
So to prevent anything happening that terrible
Let's give everybody we see and like a good hard bite right
    now,
To see what they are, because it's time for lunch!

Taking a Walk with You

My misunderstandings: for years I thought 'muso bello'
    meant 'Bell Muse', I thought it was a kind of
Extra reward on the slotmachine of my shyness in the snow
    when
February was only a bouncing ball before the Hospital of
    the Two Sisters of the Last
Hamburger Before I Go to Sleep. I thought Axel's Castle
    was a garage;
And I had beautiful dreams about it, too – sensual, mys-
    terious mechanisms; horns honking, wheels turning . . .
My misunderstandings were:
1) thinking Pinocchio could really change from a puppet
    into a real boy, and back again!
2) thinking it depended on whether he was good or bad!
3) identifying him with myself!
4) and therefore every time I was bad being afraid I would
    turn into wood . . .
5) I misunderstood childhood. I usually liked the age I was.
    However, now I regard twenty-nine as an optimum age
    (for me).
6) I disliked Shelley between twenty and twenty-five.
All of these things I suppose are understandable, but
When you were wearing your bodice I did not understand
    that you had nothing on beneath it;
When my father turned the corner I misunderstood the
    light very much
On Fifty-fifth Street; and I misunderstood (like an old
    Chinese restaurant) what he was doing there.
I misunderstand generally Oklahoma and Arkansas,
    though I think I understand New Mexico;
I understand the Painted Desert, cowboy hats, and vast
    spaces; I do

Not understand hillbilly life – I am sure I misunderstand it.
I did not understand that you had nothing on beneath your
    bodice
Nor, had I understood this, would I have understood what
    it meant; even now I
(Merry Christmas! Here, Father, take your package)
    misunderstand it!
Merry Christmas, Uncle Leon! yes, here is your package
    too.

I misunderstand Renaissance life; I misunderstand:
The Renaissance;
Ancient China;
The Middle Atlantic States and what they are like;
The tubes of London and what they mean;
Titian, Michelangelo, Vermeer;
The origins of words;
What others are talking about;
Music from the beginnings to the present time;
Laughter; and tears, even more so;
Value (economic and esthetic);
Snow (and weather in the country);
The meaning of the symbols and myths of Christmas.
I misunderstand you,
I misunderstand the day we walked down the street to-
    gether for ten hours –
Where were we going? I had thought we were going some-
    where. I believe I misunderstand many of the places we
    passed and things you said . . .
I misunderstand 'Sons of Burgundy',
I misunderstand that you had nothing painted beneath
    your bodice,
I misunderstand 'Notification of Arrival or Departure to
    Be Eradicated Before Affection of Deceased Tenant.'

I understand that
The smoke and the clouds are both a part of the day, but

I misunderstand the words 'After Departure',
I misunderstand nothingness;
I misunderstand the attitude of people in pharmacies, on
the decks of ships, in my bedroom, amid the pine
needles, on mountains of cotton, everywhere –
When they say paralytic I hear parasite, and when they say
coffee I think music . . .
What is wrong with me from head to toe
That I misinterpret everything I hear? I misunderstand:
French: often;
Italian: sometimes, almost always – for example, if some-
one says, 'Fortunate ones!' I am likely to think he is
referring to the fountain with blue and red water (I am
likely to make this mistake also in English).
I misunderstand Greek entirely;
I find ancient Greece very hard to understand: I probably
misunderstand it;
I misunderstand spoken German about 98% of the time,
like the cathedral in the middle of a town;
I misunderstand 'Beautiful Adventures'; I also think I
probably misunderstand *La Nausée* by Jean-Paul Sartre . . .
I probably misunderstand misunderstanding itself – I
misunderstand the Via Margutta in Rome, or Via della
Vite, no matter what street, all of them.
I misunderstand wood in the sense of its relationship to
the tree; I misunderstand people who take one attitude
or another about it . . .
Spring I would like to say I understand, but I most probably don't – autumn, winter, and summer are all in the
same boat
(Ruined ancient cities by the sea).

I misunderstand *vacation* and *umbrella*,
I misunderstand *motion* and *weekly*
(Though I think I understand 'Daytime Pissarros'
And the octagon – I do not understand the public garden) . . .

Oh I am sure there is a use for all of them, but what is it?
My misunderstandings confuse Rome and Ireland, and
    can you
Bring that beautiful sex to bear upon it?
I misunderstand what I am saying, though not to you;
I misunderstand a large boat: that is a ship.
What you are feeling for me I misunderstand totally; I
    think I misunderstand the very possibilities of feeling,
Especially here in Rome, where I somehow think I am.
I see the sky, and sails.
(I misunderstand the mustard and the bottle)
Oh that we could go sailing in that sky!

What tune came with the refreshments?
I am unable to comprehend why they were playing off key.
Is it because they wanted us to jump over the cliff
Or was one of them a bad or untrained musician
Or the whole lot of them?
At any rate
San Giovanni in Laterano
Also resisted my questioning
And turned a deaf blue dome to me
Far too successfully.

I cannot understand why you walk forwards and backwards
    with me.
I think it is because you want to try out your shoes for their
    toes.
It is Causation that is my greatest problem

And after that the really attentive study of millions of details.
I love you, but it is difficult to stop writing.
As a flea could write the Divine Comedy of a water jug.
   Now Irish mists close in upon us.
Peat sails through the air, and greenness becomes bright.
   Are you the ocean or the island? Am I on Irish soil, or
   are your waves covering me?
St Peter's bells are ringing: 'Earthquake, inundation, and
   sleep to the understanding!'
(American Express! flower vendors! your beautiful straight
   nose! that delightful trattoria in Santa Maria in Tras-
   tevere!)
Let us have supper at Santa Maria in Trastevere
Where by an absolute and total misunderstanding (but not
   fatal) I once ate before I met you.
I am probably misinterpreting your answer, since I hear
   nothing, and I believe I am alone.

The Departure from Hydra

As I was walking home just now, from seeing
Margaret and Norris off (though Peter,
An Englishman whom Norris had met yesterday,
Went back to change his clothes, and missed the boat)
As I came home along the little street
Without a name on which the only theatre,
The movie theatre, on Hydra is,
Called 'The Gardenia' or just plain 'Gardenia',
The street which they today are tearing up
And carrying new stones in to replace
The ones they're tearing up, though it may be
They are the same stones, put in different order
Or in a different way, as I was walking,
With the heat of the day just over, at five-thirty,
I felt quite good, but then felt an awareness
Of something in my legs that might be painful
And then of some slight tension in my jaws
And slight pains in my head; instead of despairing
And giving all thought of pleasure up, I felt
That if I could write down all that I felt
As I came walking there, that that would be
A pleasure also, and with solidity.
I passed a mule – some men were loading up
His fellow-mule with packets – and I stared
At his wide eyes and his long hard flat nose
Or face, at which he turned away his eyes
And stamped his right hoof nervously. I felt
Guilty, a member of a higher species
Deliberately using my power against
A natural inferior because
Really I was afraid that he might kick
When I came past; but when he seemed upset

Then I felt guilty. Then I looked ahead
And saw a view of houses on the hill,
Particularly noticing one red one
And thinking, Yes, that is a part of what
I feel, of the variety of this walk;
Then my mind blurred somewhat, I turned and came
Down this small narrow alley to my home.
As I came in, reviewing the ideas
Which had occurred to me throughout my walk,
It suddenly came to me that maybe Peter
Had missed the Athens boat deliberately;
After all, Margaret was not sure that she
Wanted to accompany him and Norris
On a walking trip on Poros, and Norris had said
He wanted to stay with Margaret, so that Peter
Was disappointed, since he and Norris had planned
That very morning to take such a walking trip,
And he, Peter, had been the most excited
Of all, about it. But now since Margaret and Norris
Were going into Athens, what was there for Peter
To do, why should he take the boat at all,
Even though he'd planned to, to stop at Poros?
Except, of course, to act on some marginal chance
That Norris might get off with him and walk,
Or on the strength of previous expectations,
Emotional impetus lingering. If not,
Perhaps his going to change was just an excuse
To avoid an actual confrontation with Norris
In which he would have to say, 'No, I'm not going
Unless you'll come on the walking trip!' but he knew,
Peter, that Norris wanted to stay with Margaret
And that therefore speaking to him would only result
In a little pain and confusion, since both were quite drunk,
Having planned their trip to Poros over beer all morning;

And also, of course, it might result in his getting,
In spite of himself, on the boat, by the talk confused
And not thinking clearly (whereas if he walked away
He had only, really, to wait till the boat had left –
Then he could come back down and think it over,
Surely to find he didn't regret too much
Not getting the boat, because after all the reason
He'd wanted to take the boat had long been gone).
For a human situation often leads
People to do things that they don't desire
At all, but they find that what they did desire
Has somehow led them to this situation
In which not to do that which is proposed
Seems inconsistent, hostile, or insane,
Though much more often very unfriendly; then too
Sometimes it chiefly is a lack of time
To explain how things have changed that leads one, waving
One's hands, aboard a ship that bodes one ill.
To walk away as Peter did is one way
Of avoiding such situations – another way
Is never to deceive or have high hopes
For foolish things; to be straight with oneself,
With one's own body, nature, and society,
To cast off everything that is not clear
And definite, and move toward one desire
After another, with no afterthoughts.
Living in this way one avoids the sudden
Transports of excitement Peter felt
When Norris mentioned a Poros walking tour.
For surely if Peter's natural desires
Had all been satisfied, if his life were running
Smoothly sexually, and if his health
Were excellent and his work going well,
He scarcely would have gotten so excited

At the mere thought of walking around Poros;
This sort of thing, however, often happens
To people from Northern countries, not just Peter,
And perhaps if one is English, Norse, or Swedish,
Danish, Finnish, Swiss, or North American,
One cannot avoid a certain amount of tension,
A certain quavering in the hand which reaches
For a ripe peach or the shoulder of a girl,
One whom, as one walks back from going swimming,
One thinks that one could eat, she's so delicious,
But only thinks it for a little while
(This thought itself is such a Northern one!
A Southerner would think about a place
Where he could go and jump on top of her) –
In any case, then, Northerners find it hard
To avoid such sudden excitements, but the English,
And especially the upper class, are worst of all,
Because besides their climate that's oppressed them
There's also been a restrictive upbringing,
Manners around the house perhaps too severe
For children – I am speaking of those English
Who escape from 'class' and become bright or artistic,
The ones one sees on places like this island.
(These sudden outbursts of enthusiasm, of course,
Are often much admired by other people,
Particularly some not very smart ones,
Who think however they're very sensitive
And what they most admire is 'vitality'
Which they think things like outbursts are a sign of,
And they can bore you far into the night
With telling you how wonderful some Dane
Or Norsky is, when you could be asleep
Dreaming of satisfying your desires
With persons who are always very warm,

Tender, and exciting – but, awake!
They're talking still, and though your sickly smile
Gets sicklier every moment, they go on:
'Hans suddenly got the idea to
Inundate Denmark. He is wonderful!'
'Oh, marvelous! Where does one go to meet him?'
'I'll give you his address. He has a farm
Where he stays in the summer; he loves animals,
But sometimes when he drinks a lot he beats them
And says that he can understand their language.'
'How marvelous!' 'And here's his city address:
Beschtungen aber Bass Gehundenweiss
996.' 'Goodnight.' But Peter is
Not an exaggerated case like that,
And not a nagging bore who talks of such
People, but he has 'outbursts' all the same.
It is true, in a sense these outbursts are
Difficult to discriminate from real
Vitality, which everyone esteems
These days because of man's oppressed position
In modern society, which saps his strength
And makes him want to do what everyone else does,
Whereas some man who says, 'Let's pitch the glasses
Against the lamppost' is likely to be praised
By some low-IQ person who is there
As being really vital, ah he's wonderful.
Vitality, however, usually
Appeals to an answering vital force in others
And brings about making love or great events,
Or it at least gives pleasure – I can't judge
Vitality in any way but the way
It gives me pleasure, for if I do not get
Pleasure from life, of which vitality
Is just the liquid form, then what am I

And who cares what I say? I for one don't.
Therefore I judge vitality that way.)
But Peter, after having this idea
Of a walking trip on Poros, must have felt
That in walking around in the sun all day on an island
About which he knew nothing, there might come
Some insight to him or some relaxation,
Some feeling the way an Italian feels all the time,
Or perhaps not, perhaps he never does;
Peter at any rate was probably not
Conscious of an Italian at the time
He thought with pleasure about the walk on Poros,
But there he was, faced with Norris and Margaret
An hour before the boat came in, and Norris
Was saying 'Maybe not.' One mistake of Peter,
Or, rather, difficulty, a common one
In such enthusiasms, is that since
One's enthusiasm is motivated by submerged
Feelings and so its object isn't clear
To anyone, it is most likely that
Though they respond excitedly at first,
Partly because excitement is so communicable,
Others, when they think over what you've planned,
Will see it in a greyer light, unless of course
They have the same neuroses that you have,
In which case a whole lifetime might be built
Upon one of these outbursts. Norris, probably,
In drinking with Peter, wanted more than anything
To be agreeable, whereas Peter wanted
To 'do' something unusual, not necessarily
Pleasing to Norris, not necessarily displeasing;
Norris, I should imagine, then, once he
Was out of Peter's company, since he'd known him
A very short time, was lacking the chief impulse

That motivated him when he agreed
To take a tour with Peter; therefore Margaret,
Speaking to Norris when he was alone
And saying she did not want to take the trip,
Found he immediately agreed with her,
Expressed some doubts at least, and said all right,
The trip was off then, he'd explain to Peter;
Peter, of course was very surprised by this,
But still he must have been used to it because
The way that Norris and Margaret acted was based
On laws of human conduct which endure;
And since that outburst surely was not his first,
Peter was probably accustomed to
That sort of outcome of his impulses
And said to himself, 'Ah, they don't understand,'
But probably knew inside that there was something
Seriously the matter with him. So when he left
The table and said, 'I'm going to get my things,'
It was with a certain tension that he left,
Indicative of the fact he'd not come back,
And of the fact that he knew he would not avoid
Self-doubts because he avoided the useless boat trip;
Of course he wouldn't think he should have gone
But wonder why things had been the way they were.
It was these deeper worries in his mind,
I think, that kept him from leaving even sooner
With the same excuse, rather than a hope that Norris
Would change his mind again. Deep thoughts make help-
    less
Men for small undertakings. Well, perhaps
The last is speculation, but the rest
Seems surely true. I smiled, and closed the door.

The Pleasures of Peace

Another ribald tale of the good times at Madame Lipsky's.

Giorgio Finogle had come in with an imitation of the latest Russian poet,

The one who wrote the great 'Complaint About the Peanut Farm' which I read to you last year at Mrs Riley's,

Do you remember? and then of course Giorgio had written this imitation

So he came in with it ... Where was I and what was I saying?

The big beer parlor was filled with barmaids and men named Stuart

Who were all trying to buy a big red pitcher of beer for an artiste named Alma Stuart

Whom each claimed as his very own because of the similarity in names –

This in essence was Buddy's parody – O Giorgio, you idiot, Marian Stuart snapped,

It all has something to do with me! But no, Giorgio replied,

Biting in a melancholy way the edge off a cigar-paper-patterned envelope

In which he had been keeping the Poem for many days

Waiting to show it to his friends. And actually it's not a parody at all,

I just claimed it was, out of embarrassment. It's a poetic present for you all,

All of whom I love! Is it capable to love more than one – I wonder! Alma cried,

And we went out onto the bicycle-shaped dock where a malicious swarm of mosquitoes

Were parlaying after having invaded the old beer parlor.

The men named Stuart were now involved in a fight to the death

But the nearer islands lay fair in the white night light.
Shall we embark toward them? I said, placing my hand
    upon one exceedingly gentle
And fine. A picture of hairnets is being projected. Here
Comes someone with Alma Stuart! Is it real, this night?
    Or have we a gentle fantasy?
The Russian poet appears. He seems to consider it real all
    right. He's
Quite angry. Where's the Capitalist fairy that put me
    down? he squirts
At our nomadic simplicity. 'Complaint About the Peanut
    Farm' is a terrific poem. Yes,
In a way, yes. The Hairdresser of Night engulfs them all in
    foam.

'I love your work, *The Pleasures of Peace*,' the Professor
    said to me next day;
'I think it adequately encompasses the hysteria of our era
And puts certain people in their rightful place. Chapeau!
    Bravo!'
'You don't get it,' I said. 'I like all this. I called this poem
Pleasures of Peace because I'm not sure they will be lasting!
I wanted people to be able to see what these pleasures are
That they may come back to them.' 'But they are all so
    hysterical, so – so transitory,'
The critic replied. 'I mean, how can you – what kind of
    pleasures are these?
They seem more like pains to me – if I may say what I
    mean.'
'Well, I don't know, Professor,' I said; 'permanent joys
Have so far been denied this hysterical person. Though I
    confess
Far other joys I've had and will describe in time.

And then too there's the pleasure of *writing* these – perhaps
   to experience is not the same.'
The Professor paused, lightly, upon the temple stair.
'I will mention you among the immortals, Ken,' he said,
'Because you have the courage of what you believe.
But there I will never mention those sniveling rats
Who only claim to like these things because they're
   fashionable.'
'Professor!' I cried, 'My darling! my dream!' And she
   stripped, and I saw there
Creamy female marble, the waist and thighs of which I
   had always dreamed.
'Professor! Loved one! why the disguise?' 'It was a test,'
   she said,
'Of which you have now only passed the first portion.
You must write More, and More – '
'And be equally persuasive?' I questioned, but She
Had vanished through the Promontory door.

So now I must devote my days to The Pleasures of Peace –
To my contemporaries I'll leave the Horrors of War,
They can do them better than I – each poet shares only a
   portion
Of the vast Territory of Rhyme. Here in Peace shall I stake
   out
My temporal and permanent claim. But such silver as I find
I will give to the Universe – the gold I'll put in other
   poems.
Thus in time there'll be a mountain range of gold
Of considerable interest. Oh may you come back in time
And in my lifetime to see it, most perfect and most delec-
   table reader!
We poets in our youth begin with fantasies,
But then at least we think they may be realities –

The poems we create in our age
Require your hand upon our shoulder, your eye on our
page.

Oh Norman Robinson, the airplane, the village, the bat-
teries,
All this I remember, the Cheese-o-Drome, the phallic
whips, the cucumbers,
The ginger from Australia, the tiny whorehouses no bigger
than a phallus's door,
The evenings without any cucumbers, the phallus's people,
The old men trailing blue lassos from door to door,
Who are they all, anyway? I was supposed to be on my
way to Boston
To go to college or get elected to the Legislature
And now I'm here with a lot of cowboys who talk spiritual
Dutch! Let
Me out of here! The lumberyard smelled of the sweet
calla lilies
The courtyard was fragrant with thyme. I released your hand
And walked into the Mexicana Valley, where my father
was first a cowboy.
I take a genuine interest in the people of this country
Yes sir I think you might even call me Coleman the Dutch
but now the night sky fills with fairies
It is all that modern stuff beginning to happen again,
well, let it –
We robots tell the truth about old Gabby
But when the shirtfront scuffs we yell for Labby
It is a scientific stunt
Which Moonlight has brought you from Australia
Sit it down on this chair shaped like a pirate
When you have come three times I will give you a silver-
ware hazelnut

With which you can escape from time
For this I'm calling in all the poets who take dope
To help me out, here they come
Oh is there room in the universe for such as we?
They say, but though we cannot make our Time
Stand still, yet we'll him silver like a Dime.
Inversions yet! and not even sexual ones!
O Labrador, you are the sexual Pennsylvania of our times!

Chapter Thirty Seven.
On the Planisphere everyone was having a nut
When suddenly my Lulu appeared.
She was a big broad about six feet seven
And she had a red stone in her ear
Which was stringent in its beauty.
I demanded at once the removal of people from the lobby
So we could begin to down ABC tablets and start to feel
    funny
But Mordecai La Schlomp our Leader replied that we did
    not need any
That a person could feel good without any artificial means.

If I love you, a mother bird says to the whalebird's father,
It's not because I want you to be untrue to Mrs Senior
    Whalebird, now you really know that don't you?
You – treacherous bitch! shouted the enraged Whalebird
    leaping onto her painted nylon pajamas
With his oriental feet until she screamed and bejibbered
And the cast-filled eye of the moon sinks into the sea
Sometimes wandering along this coast a lonely Indian boy
Would begin to cry for his mamma, and a wandering star
Would spurt in sympathy
Some silver come into the shiny sea.

Good night, Frank Robinson
And Gypsy Rose Lee,
I am tired and I want to lie down.
All day I have walked along this deliberate coastline
Trying as hard as I could to write everything down -
And now you see what has come of it, I mean one star,
I mean one star and all that is left in the cupboard
Is one violet couplet of lights.
Perhaps if you could agree
To step out of that coat . . .

Here are listed all the Pleasures of Peace that there could
    possibly be.
Among them are the pleasures of Memory (which Delmore
    Schwartz celebrated), the pleasures of autonomy,
The pleasures of agoraphobia and the sudden release
Of the agoraphobic person from the identified market-
    place, the pleasures of roving over you
And rolling over the beach, of being in a complicated car,
    of sleeping,
Of drawing ropes with you, of planning a deranged comic
    strip, of shifting knees
At the accelerator pump, of blasphemy, of cobra settlement
    in a dilapidated skin country
Without clops, and therefore every pleasure is also in-
    cluded; which, after these -

Oh the Pleasures of Peace are infinite and they cannot be
    counted -
One single piece of pink mint chewing gum contains more
    pleasures
Than the whole rude gallery of war! And the moon passes by
In an otherwise undistinguished lesson on the geography
    of this age

Which has had fifty-seven good lovers and ninety-six
    wars. By Giorgio Finogle.

It turns out that we're competing for the Peace Award,
Giorgio Finogle and I. We go into the hair parlor, the
    barber –
We get to talking about war and about peace.
The barber feels that we are really good people at heart
Even though his own views turn out to be conservative.
'I've read Finogle's piece, the part of it that was in *Smut*,' he
Says, 'and I liked it. Yours, Koch, I haven't yet seen,
But Alyne and Francie told me that you were the better
    poet.'
'I don't know,' I said. 'Giorgio is pretty good.' And
    Giorgio comes back from the bathroom
Now, with a grin on his face. 'I've got an idea for my
Pleasures of Peace,' he says; 'I'm going to make it include
Each person in the universe discussing their own bag –
Translation, their main interest, and what they want to
    be – '
'You'll never finish it, Giorgio,' I said. 'At least I'll
Get started,' he replied, and he ran out of the barbershop.

In the quiet night we take turns riding horseback and
    falling asleep.
Your breasts are more beautiful than a gold mine.
I think I'll become a professional man.
The reason we are up-to-date is we're some kind of freaks.
I don't know what to tell the old man
But he is concerned with two kinds of phenomena and I
    am interested in neither. What *are* you interested in?
Being some kind of freaks, I think. Let's go to Transyl-
    vania.
I don't understand your buddy all the time. Who?

The one with HANDLEBAR written across his head.
He's a good guy, he just doesn't see the difference between
    a man and a bike. If I love you
It's because you belong to and have a sublime tolerance
For such people. Yes, but in later life, I mean –
It is Present Life we've got to keep up on the screen,
Isn't it. Well yes, she said, but –
I am very happy that you are interested in it. The French
    poodle stopped being Irish entirely
And we are all out of the other breeds.
The society woman paused, daintily, upon the hotel stair.
No, I must have a poodle, said she; not an Irish setter
Would satisfy me in my mad passion for the poodle
    breeds!
As usual, returning to the bed
I find that you are inside it and sound asleep. I smile
    happily and look at your head.
It is regular-size and has beautiful blonde hair all around it.
Some is lying across the pillow. I touch it with my feet
Then leap out the window into the public square,
And I tune my guitar.

'O Mistress Mine, where are you roving?' That's my tune!
    roars Finogle, and he
Comes raging out of the *Beefsteak* – I was going to put
    that in MY Pleasures of Peace.
Oh normal comportment! even you too I shall include in
    the Pleasures of Peace,
And you, relative humidity five hundred and sixty-two
    degrees!
But what of you, poor sad glorious aqueduct
Of boorish ashes made by cigarettes smoked at the Cup-
    cake
Award – And Sue Ellen Musgrove steps on one of my feet.

'Hello!'
She says. 'You're that famous COKE, aren't you,
That no one can drink? When are you going to give us
   your famous Iliad
That everyone's been talking of, I mean your Pleasures of
   Peace!'

Life changes as the universe changes, but the universe
   changes
More slowly, as bedevilments increase.
Sunlight comes through a clot for example
Which Zoo Man has thrown on the floor. It is the Night
   of the Painted Pajamas
And the Liberals are weeping for peace. The Conservatives
   are raging for it.
The Independents are staging a parade. And we are com-
   pletely naked
Walking through the bedroom for peace. I have this friend
   who had myopia
So he always had to get very close to people
And girls thought he was trying to make out –
Why didn't he get glasses? – He was a Pacifist! The Moon
   shall overcome!

Outside in the bar yard the Grecians are screaming for peace
And the Alsatians, the Albanians, the Alesians, the Rubans,
   the Aleutians,
And the Iranians, all, all are screaming for peace.
They shall win it, their peace, because I am going to help
   them!
And he leaped out the window for peace!
Headline: GIORGIO FINOGLE,
NOTED POET, LAST NIGHT LEAPED OUT
   THE WINDOW FOR PEACE.

ASIDE FROM HEAD INJURIES HIS CONDITION IS REPORTED NORMAL.

But Giorgio never was normal! Oh the horrors of peace,
I mean of peace-fighting! But Giorgio is all right,
He is still completely himself. 'I am going to throw this hospital
Bed out the window for peace,' when we see him, he says.
And, 'Well, I guess your poem will be getting way ahead of mine now,' he says
Sadly, ripping up an envelope for peace and weakly holding out his hand
For my girl, Ellen, to stroke it; 'I will no longer be the most famous poet
For peace. You will, and you know it.' 'But you jumped out the
Window, Finogle,' I said, 'and your deed shall live longer
In men's imaginations than any verse.' But he looked at the sky
Through the window's beautiful eye and he said, 'Kenneth, I have not written one word
Of my Poem for Peace for three weeks. I've struck a snarl
And that's why (I believe) I jumped out the
Window – pure poetic frustration. Now tell them all that, how
They'll despise me, oh sob sob – ' 'Giorgio,' I said, trying to calm him down but laughing
So hard I could barely digest the dinner of imagination
In which your breasts were featured as on a Popeye card
When winter has lighted the lanterns and the falls are asleep
Waiting for next day's shards, 'Giorgio,' I said, 'the pleasures – '
But hysteria transported us all.

When I awoke you were in a star-shaped muffin, I was in a
  loaf of bread
Shaped like a camera, and Giorgio was still in his hospital
  bed
But a huge baker loomed over us. One false moof and I
  die you! he said
In a murderous throaty voice and I believe in the yellow
  leaves, the
Orange, the red leaves of autumn, the tan leaves, and the
  promoted ones
Of green, of green and blue. Sometimes walking through
  an ordinary garden
You will see a bird, and the overcoat will fall from your
Shoulders, slightly, exposing one beautiful curve
On which sunbeams alighting forget to speak a single
  word
To their parent sun and are thus cut off
Without a heating unit, but need none being on your
  breast
Which I have re-christened 'Loaves' for the beginning of
  this year
In which I hope the guns won't fire any more, the baker
  sang
To his baker lady, and then he had totally disappeared.
It looks as though everyone were going to be on our
  side!

And the flowers came out, and they were on our side,
Even the yellow little ones that grow beside your door
And the huge orange ones were bending to one side
As we walked past them, I looked into your blue eyes
And I said, 'If we come out of this door
Any more, let it be to enter only this nervous paradise
Of peaceful living conditions, and if Giorgio is roped down

Let them untie him, so he can throw his hospital bed out
the door
For all we need besides peace, which is considerable, but
first we need that – '

Daredevil, Julian and Maddalo, and John L. Lewis
Are running down the stairways for peace, they are gather-
ing the ice
And throwing it in buckets, they are raising purple parasols
for peace
And on top of these old sunlight sings her song, 'New
lights, old lights again, blue lights for peace,
Red lights for the low, insulted parasol, and a few crutches
thrown around for peace' –
Oh contentment is the key
To continuing exploration of the nations and their feet;
Therefore, andiamo – the footfall is waiting in the car
And peaceful are the markets and the sneaks;
Peaceful are the Garfinkle ping-pong balls
And peaceful are the blooms beneath the sea
Peaceful are the unreserved airplane loops and the popu-
larly guided blips
Also the Robert Herrick stone sings a peaceful song
And the banana factory is getting hip, and the pigs' Easter
party too is beginning to join in a general celebration
And the women and men of old Peru and young Haifa
and ancient Japan and beautiful young rippling Lake
Tahoe
And hairy old Boston and young Freeport and young
Santo Domingo and old father Candelabra the Chieftain
of Hoboes
Are rolling around the parapets for peace, and now the
matadors are throwing in
Huge blops of canvas and the postgraduates are filling in

As grocery dates at peanut dances and the sunlight is
    filling in
Every human world canvas with huge and luminous
    pleasure gobs of peace –
And the Tintorettos are looking very purple for peace
And the oyster campus is beginning its peaceful song –

Oh let it be concluded, including the medals!
Peace will come thrusting out of the sky
Tomorrow morning, to bomb us into quietude.
For a while we can bid goodbye
To the frenesies of this poem, The Pleasures of Peace.
When there is peace we will not need anything but bread
Stars and plaster with which to begin.
Roaming from one beard to another we shall take the tin
From the mines and give it to roaring Fidel Castro.
Where Mao Tse Tung lies buried in ocean fields of sleeping
    cars
Our Lorcaesque decisions will clonk him out
And resurrect him to the rosebuddy sky
Of early evening. And the whip-shaped generals of Hanoi
Shall be taken in overcoats to visit the sky
And the earth will be gasping for joy!

'A wonder!' 'A rout!' 'No need now for any further
    poems!' 'A Banzai for peace!' 'He can speak to us all!'
And 'Great, man!' 'Impressive!' 'Something new for you,
    Ken!' 'Astounding!' 'A real
Epic!' 'The worst poem I have ever read!' 'Abominably
    tasteless!' 'Too funny!' 'Dead, man!
A cop out! a real white man's poem! a folderol of honky
    blank spitzenburger smugglerout Caucasian gyp
Of phony bourgeois peace poetry, a total shrig!' 'Terrific!'
    'I will expect you at six!'

'A lovely starry catalogue for peace!' 'Is it Shakespeare
or Byron who breathes
In the lines of his poem?' 'You have given us the Pleasures
of Peace,
Now where is the real thing?' 'Koch has studied his his-
tory!' 'Bold!' 'Stunning!' 'It touches us like leaves
Sparkling in April – but is that all there is
To his peace plea?' Well, you be the one
To conclude it, if you think it needs more – I want to end it,
I want to see real Peace again! Oh peace bams!
I need your assistance – and peace drams, distilling through
the world! peace lamps, be shining! and peace lambs,
rumble up the shore!
O Goddess, sweet Muse, I'm stopping – now show us
where you are!

And the big boats come sailing into the harbor for peace
And the little apes are running around the jungle for peace
And the day (that is, the star of day, the sun) is shining for
peace
Somewhere a moustachioed student is puzzling over the
works of Raymond Roussel for peace
And the Mediterranean peach trees are fast asleep for peace
With their pink arms akimbo and the blue plums of
Switzerland for peace
And the monkeys are climbing for coconuts and peace
The Hawaiian palm
And serpents are writhing for peace – those are snakes –
And the Alps, Mount Vesuvius, all the really big important
mountains
Are rising for peace, and they're filled with rocks – surely
it won't be long;
And Leonardo da Vinci's *Last Supper* is moving across the
monastery wall

A few micrometers for peace, and Paolo Uccello's red
    horses
Are turning a little redder for peace, and the Anglo-Saxon
    dining hall
Begins glowing like crazy, and Beowulf, Robert E. Lee,
    Sir Barbarossa, and Baron Jeep
Are sleeping on the railways for peace and darting around
    the harbor
And leaping into the sailboats and the sailboats will go on
And underneath the sailboats the sea will go on and we will
    go on
And the birds will go on and the snappy words will go on
And the tea sky and the sloped marine sky
And the hustle of beans will go on and the unserious canoe
It will all be going on in connection with you, peace, and
    my poem, like a Cadillac of wampum
Unredeemed and flying madly, will go exploding through
New cities sweet inflated, planispheres, ingenious hair, a
    camera smashing
Badinage, cerebral stands of atmospheres, unequaled,
    dreamed of
Empeacements, candled piers, fumisteries, emphatic
    moods, terrestialism's
Crackle, love's flat, sun's sweets, oh peace, to you.

Alive for an Instant

I have a bird in my head and a pig in my stomach
And a flower in my genitals and a tiger in my genitals
And a lion in my genitals and I am after you but I have a
    song in my heart
And my song is a dove
I have a man in my hands I have a woman in my shoes
I have a landmark decision in my reason
I have a death rattle in my nose I have summer in my brain
    water
I have dreams in my toes
This is the matter with me and the hammer of my mother
    and father
Who created me with everything
But I lack calm I lack rose
Though I do not lack extreme delicacy of rose petal
Who is it that I wish to astonish?
In the birdcall I found a reminder of you
But it was thin and brittle and gone in an instant
Has nature set out to be a great entertainer?
Obviously not   A great reproducer? a great Nothing?
Well I will leave that up to you
I have a knocking woodpecker in my heart and I think I
    have three souls
One for love one for poetry and one for acting out my
    insane self
Not insane but boring but perpendicular but untrue but
    true
The three rarely sing together take my hand it's active
The active ingredient in it is a touch
I am Lord Byron I am Percy Shelley I am Ariosto
I eat the bacon I went down the slide I have a thunderstorm
    in my inside I will never hate you

But how can this maelstrom be appealing? do you like
    menageries? my god
Most people want a man! So here I am
I have a pheasant in my reminders I have a goshawk in my
    clouds
Whatever is it which has led all these animals to you?
A resurrection? or maybe an insurrection? an inspiration?
I have a baby in my landscape and I have a wild rat in my
    secrets from you.

JAMES SCHUYLER

Empathy and New Year

'A notion like that of empathy inspires great distrust in us,
because it connotes a further dose of irrationalism and mysti-
cism.' – *Lévi-Strauss*

Whitman took the cars
all the way from Camden
and when he got here
or rather there, said,
'Quit quoting,' and took the next
back, through the Jersey meadows
which were that then. But
what if it is all, 'Maya,
illusion?' I
doubt it, though. Men are not
so inventive. Or
few are. Not knowing
a name for something proves nothing. Right
now it isn't raining, snowing, sleeting, slushing,
yet it is
doing something. As a matter of fact
it is raining snow. Snow
from cold clouds
that melts as it strikes.
To look out a window is to sense
wet feet. Now to infuse
the garage with a subjective state
and can't make it seem to
even if it is a little like
What the Dentist Saw
a dark gullet with gleams and red.
'You come to me at midnight'
and say, 'I can smell that after
Christmas let-down coming like a hound.'

And clarify, 'I can smell it
just like a hound does.'
So it came. It's a shame
expectations are
so often to be counted on.

New Year is nearly here
and who, knowing himself, would
endanger his desires
resolving them
in a formula? After a while
even a wish flashing by
as a thought provokes a
knock on wood so often
a little dish-like place
worn in this desk just holds
a lucky stone inherited
from an unlucky man. Nineteen-sixty-
eight: what a lovely name
to give a year. Even better
than the dogs': Wert
('. . . bird thou never . . .')
and Woofy. Personally
I am going to call
the New Year, Mutt.
Flattering it
will get you nowhere.

II

Awake at four and heard
a snowplow not rumble –
a huge beast
at its chow and wondered
is it Nineteen-sixty-eight or Nineteen-sixty-nine?

for a bit. Nineteen-sixty-eight had
such a familiar sound.
Got coffee and started
reading Darwin: so modest,
so innocent, so pleased at
the surprise that *he*
should grow up to be *him*. How
grand to begin a new
year with a new writer
you really love. A snow
shovel scrapes: it's
twelve hours later
and the sun that came
so late is almost gone
a few pink minutes and
yet the days get
longer. Coming from the
movies last night snow
had fallen in almost
still air and lay
on all so all twigs
were emboldened to
make big disclosures.
It felt warm, warm
that is for cold
the way it does
when snow falls with
wind. 'A snow picture,' you
said, under the clung-to
elms. 'worth painting.' I
said, 'The weather operator
said, "Turning tomorrow
to bitter cold." ' 'Then
the wind will veer round

to the north and blow
all of it down.' Maybe I
thought it will get cold
some other way. You
as usual were right.
It did and has. Night
and snow and the threads of life
for once seen as they are,
in ropes like roots.

JAMES SCHUYLER

In January

after Ibn Sahl

The yard has sopped into its green-grizzled self its new
year whiteness.

A dog stirs the noon-blue dark with a running shadow and
dirt smells cold and doggy

As though the one thing never seen were its frozen coupling
with the air that brings the flowers of grasses.

And a leafless beech stands wrinkled, gray and sexless – all
bone and loosened sinew – in silver glory

And the sun falls on all one side of it in a running glance,
a licking gaze, an eye-kiss

And ancient silver struck by gold emerges mossy, pinkly
lichened where the sun fondles it

And starlings, black and iridescent, march into the east
with rapid jerky steps and pecking at their shadows

A Sun Cab

goes by below
reflected across the street
in a window
four stories up
a train
sends up its
passing metal roll
through grills and gone
the more than daily Sunday

CRIMINAL NEW JERSEY
THIRSTING FLESHPOTS OF NEW YORK

buzz
horns hums and voices
a plane unravels from the Delft
a mohair thread
torn paper shadows
dry cool and gritty
laid on
buff gray-white and pink
  The dog in its
sunspot sleep
cries in a few fine high whimpers
drips of rain
in dust on glass
paint drops

FIDGET BALLS
FOR AN UPTIGHT

JAMES SCHUYLER

Shadows
fling out their feet
and step into sun
palpable and out
and motes of
who knows what
go by
up and out
of sight   Pale cornice
brokenly lighted
by light reflected
from the sunny side
a cab crosses
the sun
near the end of a street
to the river
unheard unseen
a fluent presence

Scarlet Tanager

13 May 1967

' – in the big maple
behind the willow – '
ajet with limp spring greens
lance-like, or the head of a pike
and there it flies
and there it sits
the tanager, the bright spot
in the sunny rather evil day
the red touch green
cries out for – the soldier
in 'Storm at Castelfranco'.
And the drums beat
in East 95th Street
for soldiers in a storm
no, it's only a parade.
A huge and sullen Buddha
of a man waits at the starting
with his sign DOWN WITH DOVES
kids cry cadence and a bunch
of thick short men in little hats
that announce them vets
of the War to End War
(It Floats, They Laughed, Chu Chin Chow)
look defiant at those
who go counter to them
though merely strolling home.

A couple of men jump
out of the sky
wearing flags. Someone

'described as a bystander'
gets tarred and feathered.

Embittered object of our anxious
and unworthy fears, the scapegoat
in a get up like a grackle
that a cat drags in. Glorious day
in May when by the window
a wistaria hangs its violet lights
creased with a sunny pallor
and other birds than tanagers –
fluffy balls of fluffy dung –
flit to a skirl of bagpipes
in undefoliated yards
between backs of rows of houses
and men with faces like happy fists
march in well-remembered but unpracticed step
– who would study
to forget? – or is it habit, merely,
like LOOK BEFORE YOU TURN –
waving little flags, why then why then
it's hard not to believe the marchers
march for the fun of marching
to an inward tune like Mahler's happy
happy children's song
                              drums   drums

Blue

for Yvonne Jacquette

beautiful New
York sky harder
so much than
soft walls you
see here around
it shadowy lamp
lighted plaster
smoothed by a hand
wielded trowel and
roller painted
by hand: Puerto
Rican blue pressed
tin ceiling sky
up into and on
which a white cup
(more of a mug)
falls, falls up-
ward and crack
splits into
two glazed
clay clouds

JAMES SCHUYLER

Light Blue Above

Light blue above, darker below, lightly roughened by the
stirring air and with smooth tracks on it. There goes
Reynald Hardie's lobster boat, taking a colorful load of
pleasure-seeking shoppers to Camden.

O Air
the clear, the soot-bearer, the unseen that rips
that kills and cures, that keeps
all that is empty filled, the bright invisible

into which we move like fingers into gloves
that coats our rolling home with the sweet softness
between grape and grape skin

in silent laughter in a glass pushed down
into a basin at retreating puzzled water
constrained to rise elsewhere up
the sides of the basin, of the glass
up fingers and hand and wrist

clinging to arm hair in mercurial bubbles
that detach and rise and join itself

the quick to heal
that wriggles up from hot
heat-wave pavement like teased hair

or has a wintry bit, or in the dog days saps
or is found at the bottom
of a mail box on an empty house
or in a nest between twigs, among eggs

and we go on
with it within us
upon a dust speck
in bubble air

JAMES SCHUYLER

After Joe Was at the Island

30 June 1969

a good while after, on the upstairs east sleeping porch he
used for a studio, yellow petals – sharp yellow, shiny as
lacquer – caught in the tatters of a web, on the sill to the
north, torn-out book matches with burnt heads pointing
all one way, laid in a likeness of a wood-pile (always
making something); and a pastryboard drawing board
with edge of the paper color traces; shades of sky up to
white, of leaves and needles – Allsorts – and not much
smudged rose warming, the way grass in flower sends a
terra-cotta to slide through the unmown bending, the
given – the surface of the board – its woodeness abstracted
of brown pale skies, of agitated mud rising in an unreflect-
ing creek, of dry dirt and wet shingle – the tide is full only
twice a day – and faded toward silver house shingles: or
shakes.

The Edge in the Morning

Walking to the edge with a cup of coffee,
That way, the water is blinding.
That way, the water is dusted with sleep.
That way the water shines freshly as lead smoothly curling
    under a knife.
The bay has a skin.
It swells without breaking like water brimming in a glass.
The slipping air is thin and cold and cools the cup.
Small fat gray-brown round birds in the grass bounce up
    high from shadow to shadow.
The false oats are ripened and bearded straw.
The sun strikes them.
They light up.
The quaking grass has collapsed in wire heaps.
It is not what it was.
Out of the silence an engine approaches.
There are tide lines in the cup.
In the brilliance the boat is a dark chunk, bluntly whittled.
It steadily comes nearer.
It moves across the light and turns white.
It pays out two waves that fan and roll and add their
    action to the surface friction between air and water.
The bay is 1) a continuum and 2) change.
In the boat the figure of a man is ingeniously in scale.
The crow laughs.
The engine throttles.
The boat turns.
The ripples are twisted in a knot that shatters and dissolves.
The small turbulence breaks and melts.
The engine cuts to a rale.
The figure of a man turns, steps and bends and draws out

of the dishonored and neglected grave cold blooded
fury entrapped in a lobster pot.
Carapace and claws snapping and thrashing, mottled
stormily.
Gaudy shells packed with sweet meat.
The lobsterman turns toward you a face of weathered stone
that cracks into a smile.
The price is up because the take is down.
He baits his trap and drops it in the sea.
The asthmatic purr chokes and resumes the stertorous
breathing of normalcy.
The boat goes off to grow blue with distance.
The coffee cup has found its way onto the jut of a crag the
size of a foot.
The little it holds is cold, bitter, gritty and tastes good.
The air has stopped sliding.
It is a breeze that is more like a wind.
It crumples the bay and stuffs it in a stone pocket.
The bay agitatedly tries to smooth itself out.
If it were tissue paper it would need damp and an iron.
It is a good deal more than damp.
What a lot of water.
A gull barks
A baby barks back.
Three crows go by about their dark and iridescent busi-
ness.
The sun is high enough to have its plain daily look of
someone who takes in wash.
It dries the laundry.
Suppose I found a bone in the grass and told you it is one
of Marc Bloch's?
It would not be true.
No it would not be true and the sea is not his grave.
It is his cenotaph.

'Used Handkerchiefs 5¢'

Clean used ones, of course. Also a dresser scarf, woven
with a pattern of pansies looking alternately to right and to
left; a pillow case full of carpet scraps; underdrawers of
cambric with an edging of tatting; black – shedding jet and
bugles – crêpe, as stuffed with dust and as damp, or as dry,
as the wrinkled hand of someone too old to die who dies
because to wake up this morning just slipped her mind;
bent giant postcards: Mont Pele and a fruitless wonderland
of ice prisms, clear water-diluted color chunks: blue, pink
and green; sagging brown and metal-threaded tapestry
cloth within the gothic arch of a table Motorola hiding a
speaker from which once sped Flagstad's more than
melodious shriek and, over-enunciated as plums wrapped in
papers printed 'Biscayne Farms', once trotted, like a quick
creek, the news that flaming passengers were falling from
the Hindenberg, a voice that left itself a small puddle of
kerosene on the linoleum; then there is your face, floating
up the stairs, big-eyed into the trash-and-treasures loft
from which, finally, dressed for tennis as you came, you
go down again with a find in hand: a slab of undyed linen
its silverness yellowing like a teaspoon from egg yolk,
ironed with too cool an iron so the washing crush marks
make a pattern over the weave and, above the thick welt
of the hem, a cross-stitched border of spruce and juniper
unstylized (unless style is simply to choose) in shades of
drab that sink in, or emerge from: the handtowel of today,
embroidered forty some maybe years ago.

JAMES SCHUYLER

Light from Canada

for Charles North

A wonderful freshness, air
that billows like bedsheets
on a clothesline and the clouds
hang in a traffic jam: summer
heads home. Evangeline,
our light is scoured and Nova
Scotian and of a clarity that
opens up the huddled masses
of the stolid spruce so you
see them in their bristling
individuality. The other
day, walking among them, I
cast my gaze upon the ground
in hope of orchids and,
pendant, dead, a sharp shadow
in the shade, a branch gouged
and left me 'scarred forever
'neath the eye'. Not quite. Not
the cut, but the surprise, and
how, when her dress caught fire,
Longfellow's wife spun
into his arms and in the dying
of its flaring, died. The
irreparable, which changes
nothing that went before
though it ends it. Above the wash
and bark of rumpled water, a gull
falls down the wind to dine
on fish that swim up to do same.

Closed Gentian Distances

A nothing day full of
wild beauty and the
timer pings. Roll up
the silver off the bay
take down the clouds
sort the spruce and
send to laundry marked,
more starch. Goodbye
golden- and silver-
rod, asters, bayberry
crisp in elegance.
Little fish stream
by, a river in water.

Evening Wind

October hangs in grape
bunch lights among the leaves
of a giant tree whose leaves
are not unlike grape leaves:
a plane tree, or a sycamore?
The wind comes up the water
as water from a faucet
runs across a palm, the palm
of your hand, the water turned
on gently or broken into
cool molten wooly glass
by an aerator. And each
responds by his or its
own bending to it, tall tops
of hedge move all in a sideways
way, the grass (it begins
to have its matted resting
up for winter look) is freaked
by shade and quartz grit
bits of light, a pear tree
rocks at its roots and from
the eyebrow curves of branches
or under them flutters absurdly
its leaves like lashes. And I
am troubled by hatred for
the dead. Wind, you don't
blow hard enough, though
rising, in the smokey blue
of evening, mindless and in love.

Or would be if the wind
were not above such thoughts,
above thought, in fact
of course, though coursing,
cool as water, through it.

A Penis Moon

twas the night before Columbus Day, '70
and the humidity gave a semblance
of warmth to a day not unchilly, even somewhat clammy.
Some listless starlings pecked in a lackluster way
among the leaf litter: from elms, which crumble in the
    stillness as you look.

A cloud kissed me.
The moon came up like a white spitz
going downtown to get the paper.
A rabbit named Spatsy hops in its cage.
He is eating a pear.
I had a thought, that life should not have uses
saying, 'But what *good* is it?' just
'accept with pleasure'ness
then I saw a face

and what use is it, hankering
for what you can't won't ever have?
Here is the spitz, back from Silver's
with the paper. It is the wrong paper.
Shall we beat the dog, or praise him?
Reading of discoveries by wooly moonlight,
it rises today, attentive as one rabbit ear.

Verge

A man cuts brush
and piles it
for a fire where
fireweed will flower
maybe, one day.
All the leaves
are down except
the ones that aren't.
They shake or
a wind shakes
them but they
won't go oh
no there goes
one now. No.
It's a bird
batting by.
The small lake,
shrunk, shivers
like a horse
twitching off
flies. Flies
drunkenly stagger
between window
and storm sash.
They hatch, lay,
buzz and die.
The sky grows
gray, goes pale,
bears a whitlow
or splits and
shows a lining
light sea green.

But the lake
is Black. Back
of the trees
are other trees
where deer stoop
and step and
the independent skunk
securely waddles.
An unseen something
stirs and says No
snow yet but
it will snow.
The trees sneeze
You bet it
will, compiling
a white and wordless
dictionary
in which brush
cut, piled and
roofed with glitter
will catch and burn
transparently
bright in white
defining 'flame'.
So long, North.
See you later
in other weather.

Running Footsteps

A thin brown stain
down the white brick wall
I guess yes
the new roof leaks
and there are holes
drilled in the asphalt
out there where manhole
covers used to blow:
escapes for leaks. Sleet
down the chimney:
a rustle broken
into dots and dashes. Then
a midwinter downpour.
The streets are rivers
or the water streets
in a smalltown dream
'They live on Water Street
near the corner of Front Street
off Railroad Avenue.'
The current fails.
Lights go out
in parts of town. In
the slosh there are
running footsteps: has
got to go though
an act of clouds would will
otherwise. Otherwise,
had stayed where was . . . ?
Couldn't. Why?
On and off lights
prolong into surges
the chatter of

rain on rain, the up
close rats' nesting noise
in the chimney: 'It's
a good night to stay
in' so out you
go into it it's
almost like
that other night
you left holding
your breath to
descend and issue
screaming: your
tonight running
footsteps, rain
icy and loud
is a kind of
what to your
surprise is you
screaming in
fear, in rage,
instinctual
to find relief
muscular surges
running footsteps
the rain
rain-chilled
to be alive

The Dog Wants His Dinner

The sky is pitiless. I beg
your pardon? OK then
the sky is pitted. The yard
is sand and laced with roots
afloat on rock encasing fire.
You think so do you. No.
Yes. Don't know. Check one.
Forget all you ever knew.
Sorry. Not my romance. What
is? Sorry. We don't take
in trick questions. You mean?
I do: put down that.
Put that down too. Skies
of spit, seas where whales
piss and die to make a bar
of scented soap, uhm smells
good. She came in like an excited headline. The deer
they all were starving! To
death, even, perhaps. And
eating people! What to do
with these disordered herds
of words? I said I would
eat my words and do so, now
you see. He eats them, all
up. Greedily. Yesterday the
air was squeaky clean today
it's dull and lifeless as an
addict's armpit. Surely you
mean leafless. I have a flea
bite, here, pink, of course
as an eye disease: the cat

who brings me fleas dies
like a dog, sleepily, or
an unwatered plant. That
was exciting wasn't it. It's
not that I crave. Uh did
you say crave? Some words
are briefly worse than others
get the Librium gun and point
it and the Kodak at that Kodiak.
You see? No hope. So don't
hope. Hop, skip, jump or
lie down. Feed your face.
Now feed the dog. He ate his.
He is eating the cat who
objects. Fix the fire. Put
out the light. An ice cold
hand slides in the window
to touch your uncovered head
forehead cheeks lips lobes
and all with worlds of fire
chilled by distance. O night.
Bedclothes loosen. Unseen twigs
erect themselves in air. You
asleep too, O magic root.

The Crystal Lithium

The smell of snow, stinging in nostrils as the wind lifts it
    from a beach
Eye-shuttering, mixed with sand, or when snow lies under
    the street lamps and on all
And the air is emptied to an uplifting gasiness
That turns lungs to winter waterwings, buoying, and the
    bright white night
Freezes in sight a lapse of waves, balsamic, salty, un-
    expected:
Hours after swimming, sitting thinking biting at a hang
    nail
And the taste of the – to your eyes – invisible crystals
    irradiates the world
'The sea is salt'
'And so am I'
'Don't bite your nails'

                    and the metal flavor of a nail – are
                    these brads ? –

Taken with a slight spitting motion from between teeth
    and whanged into place
(Boards and sawdust) and the nailset is ridged with cold
Permanently as marble, always degrees cooler than the
    rooms of air it lies in
Felt as you lay your cheek upon the counter on which sits
    a blue-banded cup
A counter of condensed wintry exhalations glittering
    infinitesimally
A promise, late on a broiling day in late September, of the
    cold kiss
Of marble sheets to one who goes barefoot quickly in the
    snow and early

Only so far as the ash can – bang, dump – and back and
   slams the door:
Too cold to get up though at the edges of the blinds the sky
Shows blue as flames that break on a red sea in which black
   coals float:
Pebbles in a pocket embed the seam with grains of sand
Which as they will have found their way into a pattern
   between foot and bedfoot
'A place for everything and everything in its place' how
   wasteful, how wrong
It seems when snow in fat, hand-stuffed flakes falls slow
   and steady in the sea
'Now you see it, now you don't' the waves growl as they
   grind ashore and roll out
At your feet (in boots) a Christmas tree naked of needles
Still wound with swags of tarnishing tinsel, faintly alarming
   as the thought
Of damp electricity or sluggish lightning and for your
   health desiring pains
The wind awards: Chapped Lips: on which to rub Time's
   latest acquisition
Tinned, dowel shaped and inappropriately flavored sheep
   wool fat
A greasy sense-eclipsing fog 'I can't see
Without my glasses' 'You certainly can't see with them all
   steamed up
Like that. Pull over, park and wipe them off.' The thunder
   of a summer's day
Rolls down the shimmering blacktop and mowed grass
   juice thickens the air
Like 'Stir until it coats the spoon, remove from heat, let
   cool and chill'
Like this, graying up for more snow, maybe, in which a
   small flock

Of – sparrows? – small, anyway, dust kitty-colored birds
    fly up
On a dotted diagonal and there, ah, is the answer:
Starlings, bullies of birdland, lousing up
The pecking order, respecters of no rights (what bird is)
    unloved (oh?)
Not so likeable as some: that's temperate enough and the
    temperature
Drops to rise to snowability of a softness even in its scent
    of roses
made of untinted butter frosting: Happy Name Day, Blue
    Jay, staggering
On slow-up wings into the shrunk into itself from cold
    forsythia snarl
And above these thoughts there waves another tangle but
    one parched with heat
And not with cold although the heat is on because of cold
    settled all
About as though, swimming under water, in clearly fishy
    water, you
Inhaled and found one could and live and also found you
    altogether
Did not like it, January, laid out on a bed of ice, dis-
    gorging
February, shaped like a flounder, and March with her steel
    bead pocketbook,
And April, goofy and under-dressed and with a loud laugh,
    and May
Who will of course be voted Miss Best Liked (she expects
    it),
And June, with a toothpaste smile, fresh from her flea
    bath, and gross July,
Flexing itself, and steamy August, with thighs and eyes to
    match, and September

Diving into blue October, dour November, and deadly
    dull December which now

And then with a surprised blank look produces from its
    hand the ace of trumps

Or sets within the ice white hairline of a new moon the
    gibbous rest:

Global, blue, Columbian, a blue dull definite and thin as the
    first day

Of February when, in the steamed and freezing capital
    cash built

Without a plan to be its own best monument its skyline
    set in stacks

Like poker chips (signed, 'Autodidact'), at the crux of a
    view there crosses

A flatcar-trailer piled with five of the cheaper sort of
    yachts, tarpaulined,

Plus one youth in purple pants, a maid in her uniform
    and an 'It's not real

Anything' Cossack hat and coat, a bus one-quarter full of
    strangers and

The other familiar fixings of lengthening short days: 'He's
    outgrown them

Before you can turn around' and see behind you the land-
    scape of the past

Where beached boats bask and terraced cliffs are hung with
    oranges

Among dark star-gleaming leaves, and, descending the
    dizzying rough stairs

Littered with goat turd beads – such packaging – you – he
    – she –

One – someone – stops to break off a bit of myrtle and
    recite all the lines

Of Goethe that come back, and those in French, '*Connais-
tu* . . . ?' the air

Fills with chalk dust from banged erasers, behind the
    February dunes
Ice boats speed and among the reeds there winds a little
    frozen stream
Where kids in kapok ice skate and play at Secret City as the
    sun
Sets before dinner, the snow on fields turns pink and
    under the hatched ice
The water slides darkly and over it a never before seen
    liquefaction of the sun
In a chemical yellow greener than sulphur a flash of pet-
    roleum by-product
Unbelievable, unwanted and as lovely as though someone
    you knew all your life
Said the one inconceivable thing and then went on
    washing dishes: the sky
Flows with impersonal passion and loosening jet trails
    (eyes tearing from the cold)
And on the beach, between foam frozen in a thick scalloped
    edging so like
Weird cheek-mottling pillow case embroidery, on the
    water-darkened sand the waves
Keep free of frost a gull strangles on a length of nylon
    fish line and the dog
Trots proudly off, tail held high, to bury a future dinner
    among cut grass on a dune:
The ice boats furl their sails and all pile into cars and go off
    to the super market
Its inviting foods and cleansers sold under tunes with
    sealed in memory-flavor
'Hot House Rhubarb' 'White Rock Girl' 'Citrus Futures'
    'Cheap Bitter Beans' and
In its parking lot vast as the kiss to which is made the most
    complete surrender

In a setting of leaves, backs of stores, a house on a rise
    admired for being
Somewhat older than some others (prettier, too?) a man in
    a white apron embraces a car
Briefly in the cold with his eyes as one might hug oneself
    for warmth for love
– What a paint job, smooth as an eggplant; what a meaty
    chest, smooth as an eggplant
– Is it too much to ask your car to understand you? the
    converse isn't and the sky
Maps out new roads so that, driving at right angles to the
    wind, clouds in ranks
Contrive in diminishing perspective a part of a picture
    postcard of a painting
Over oak scrub where a filling station has: gas, a locked
    toilet (to keep dirt in)
A busted soda pop machine, no maps and 'I couldn't tell
    you *thet*' so
The sky empties itself to a color, there, where yesterday's
    puddle
Offers its hospitality to people-trash and nature-trash in
    tans and silvers
And black grit like that in corners of a room in this or that
    cheap dump
Where the ceiling light burns night and day and we stare
    at or into each
Other's eyes in hope the other reads there what he reads:
    snow, wind
lifted; black water, slashed with white; and that which is,
    which is beyond
Happiness or love or mixed with them or more than they
    or less, unchanging change
'Look,' the ocean said (it was tumbled, like our sheets),
    'look in my eyes'

Janis Joplin's Dead: Long Live Pearl

'Ever write any love poems?'

you call:
guarded voices. O
Commadore
Hotel, I like
free speech. 'Free-
dom's just
a word.' I bet
you think
I'm giving you
the old
McGee. I
ain't givin'
you nothin',
Buster: just
walk on in
and help yourself.
Set right down
and rap a while.
Take a toke.
Take two. Do
your thing. I'm puttin' on
Pearl (O Pearl) and
The In White Wrappers
(groovy group)
or *Company*. Couldn't
care
less. Not
true. Then
dig right
in and help yourself. You think

I don't mean it? Not
on your Kodachrome. Or
it's
a put on? Maybe
baby: that's
a game that two
can play
at: in fact it
takes two
and only two:
                    'holdin''

'body
next to
mine'

Eyes

seta cangiante
eyes that change
changeable as changeable
silk, silk that
refracts
as bearer walks
in sunlight
into shade
from Piazza, say,
San Marco
into suncharged
shadowy arcade
or under trees
green, green
and between
blue, blue, blue
bluest blue
eyes of un-
weavable color
human eyes, man
size: unsilken
reflections:
hazel, gray-
blue 'tea
ashes' Chinese,
ordinary eyes:
The Big Salty,
shifting restless,
under overcast;
smile, cold, half-
asleep
and deep in August

grass, elms, weeping
birches and all
green, too
green, so green
and the eyes
pick it up and
flash *il raggio verde*
the green ray
at *tramonto*
sunset flash
the red
reversal: i.e.
green

And in your eyes
your suddenly so
green eyes
the flash holds
steadily and
you smile or
I hope so: it
is not August
yet, *Occhi*
di seta cangiante

tu mi segue?

The Night

The night is filled with indecisions
To take a downer or an upper
To take a walk
To lie
Down and relax

I order you: RELAX

To face the night
Alight – or dark – the air
Conditioner
The only song:
I love you so
Right now I need you so
So tired and so upset
And yet I mustn't phone:
I didn't know
I touched a wound that never healed
A trauma: wounds will heal
And all I did
Was panic so briefly
On the phone
'Oh baby! you scared me'
No what you said
First on the phone
Was, 'Baby, I'll be right there.'
You were. You did. You
Came, it seemed, as fast
as light, you love me so.
I didn't know someone
Once hurt you so
Went suicidal: head in the oven

Threat – that
Hysteria bit. Not
My trip.
I am not suicidal
We are strong and
You know it and
Yet
I must sleep
And wait – I
   love you so
You will know
I know you do
Already know:
We love each other
So. Goodnight
My own, my love
My dear, my dearest dear,
It's true
We do we
Love each
Other so

Like Lorraine Ellison

Zéphyrine Drouhin
lines out her
Cerise Magic
in pear tree shade:
back-up group, The Persian
Double Yellows (gone,
about, over). And through the snares
sexily come saxes: through
solid shadow-green
of brushing leaves, clear
as a blues, violet sage,
flowering saxes. I
send you all the love
('Who's Zéphyrine?'
in the world
('She was a somebody
or would
(once, now
if it were mine
(she is
to
(a rose'
give

Letter Poem #2

Riding along in the beautiful day (there go two
blue enamel silos), half-reading about marvelous
Chamfort, thinking of 'my own, my dearest', and
among other you thoughts –

   White clouds in blue above the birches
   You too are like my head, filled with
   And adrift in love, which is the sap
   That rises, stiffening these trees

Letter Poem #3

The night is quiet
as a kettle drum
the bull frog basses
tuning up. After
swimming, after sup-
per, a Tarzan movie,
dishes, a smoke. One
planet and I
wish. No need
of words. Just
you, or rather,
us. The stars tonight
in pale dark space
are clover flowers
in a lawn the expanding
Universe in which
we love it is
our home. So many
galaxies and you my
bright particular,
my star, my sun, my
other self, my bet-
ter half, my one

Fabergé

'I keep my diamond necklace in a pond of sparkling water for invisibility.

'My rubies in Algae Pond are like an alligator's adenoids.

'My opals – the evening cloud slipped in my pocket and I felt it and vice versa.

'Out of all the cabs I didn't take (a bit of a saver) I paved a street with gold. It was quite a short street, sort of a dollhouse cul-de-sac.

'And there are a lot of other pretties I could tell about – ivory horses carved inside bone dice; coral monkeys too tiny to touch; a piece of jade so big you might mistake it for the tundra and a length of chalcedony as long as the Alcan Highway which is the Alcan Highway. It is solidified liquid chalcedony.

'Here, just for you, is a rose made out of a real rose and the dewdrop nestled in a rosy petal that has the delicate five-o'clock-shadow fuzz – blue – is not a tear. I have nothing to cry about now I have you.'

A White City

My thoughts turn south
a white city
we will wake in one another's arms.
I wake
and hear the steampipe knock
like a metal heart
and find it has snowed.

JAMES SCHUYLER

December

Il va neiger dans quelques jours – *Francis Jammes*

The giant Norway spruce from Podunk, its lower branches
          bound,
this morning was reared into place at Rockefeller Center.
I thought I saw a cold blue dusty light sough in its boughs
the way other years the wind thrashing at the giant orna-
          ments
recalled other years and Christmas trees more homey.
Each December! I always think I hate 'the over-commer-
          cialized event'
and then bells ring, or tiny light bulbs wink above the
          entrance
to Bonwit Teller or Katherine going on five wants to look
          at all
the empty sample gift-wrapped boxes up Fifth Avenue in
          swank shops
and how can I help falling in love? A calm secret exulta-
          tion
of the spirit that tastes like Sealtest eggnog, made from
          milk solids,
Vanillin, artificial rum flavoring; a milky impulse to kiss
          and be friends.
It's like what George and I were talking about, the East
          West
Coast divide: Californians need to do a thing to enjoy it.
A smile in the street may be loads! you don't have to un-
          dress everybody.
          'You didn't *visit* the Alps?'
          'No, but I saw from the train they were black
          and streaked with snow.'
Having and giving but also catching glimpses

hints that are revelations: to have been so happy is a
        promise
and if it isn't kept that doesn't matter. It may snow
falling softly on lashes of eyes you love and a cold cheek
grow warm next to your own in hushed dark familial
        December.

Ilford Rose Book

Thank you for your letter
and its extenuations. 'He
said to tell them it is they
not he who said
a drawing can be illustrationy.'
Another night. The grass
yellower. And the elms close in.
Flaming gray to the west
a blinding shadow. Dusty Easter
eggs, an ashtray no one
will wash, Dad
with all his buttons on
back in the watch fob days.

A Man in Blue

Under the French horns of a November afternoon
a man in blue is raking leaves
with a wide wooden rake (whose teeth are pegs
or rather, dowels). Next door
boys play soccer: 'You got to start
over!' sort of. A round attic window
in a radiant gray house waits like a kettledrum.
'You got to start . . .' The Brahmsian day
lapses from waltz to march. The grass,
rough-cropped as Bruno Walter's hair,
is stretched, strewn and humped beneath a sycamore
wide and high as an idea of heaven
in which Brahms turns his face like a bearded thumb
and says, 'There is something I must tell you!'
to Bruno Walter. 'In the first movement
of my Second, think of it as a family
planning where to go next summer
in terms of other summers. A material ecstasy,
subdued, recollective.' Bruno Walter
in a funny jacket with a turned-up collar
says, 'Let me sing it for you.'
He waves his hands and through the vocalese-shaped spaces
of naked elms he draws a copper beech
ignited with a few late leaves. He bluely glazes
a rhododendron 'a sea of leaves' against gold grass.
There is a snapping from the brightwork
of parked and rolling cars.
There almost has to be a heaven! so there could be
a place for Bruno Walter
who never needed the cry of a baton.
Immortality –
in a small, dusty, rather gritty, somewhat scratchy

Magnavox from which a forte
drops like a used Brillo Pad?
Frayed. But it's hard to think of the sky as a thick glass floor
with thick-soled Viennese boots tromping about on it.
It's a whole lot harder thinking of Brahms
in something soft, white and flowing.
'Life,' he cries (here, in the last movement),
'is something more than beer and skittles!'
'And the something more
is a whole lot better than beer and skittles,'
says Bruno Walter,
darkly, under the sod. I don't suppose it seems so dark
to a root. Who are these men in evening coats?
What are these thumps?
Where is Brahms?
And Bruno Walter?
Ensconced in resonant plump easy chairs
covered with scuffed brown leather
in a pungent autumn that blends leaf smoke
(sycamore, tobacco, other),
their nobility wound in a finale
like this calico cat
asleep, curled up in a breadbasket,
on a sideboard where the sun falls.

April and Its Forsythia

It's snowing on the unpedimented lions. On ventilator
    hoods
white triangles. It evens up wrinkled tar roofs,
smooths out rough concrete coping, showing the shape
of a wall side between coping top and roof. The census
taker was just here. She had on transparent overshoes, coat
    and
hat: are clothes less secret? Less snowlike?
Snow isn't secret, showing further aspects, how small
cast lions could look if they grew maned, tame yet whitely
fierce; how the center of the sidewalk is always a path
steps tend to, as across a plain, through a wood; how cars
swing out heavily and big at a corner, turning volu-
    minously
as a fleshy dancer. That census taker. I'm the head of a
    household.
I am also my household. Not bad. It's still snowing, down
and across: when cloth gets old and stretched, a twill
may have a gusty, snowy movement. Rough on poor rats
who work in it, must go out in it: it's dirty cold wet slush
underfoot, you hear it under wheels: swoosh, and slop
when they stop. Mr Merzeg, the super, loves it. Used to
    drop
to 30 below the nine months he spent in Siberia. Wow.
    There
they really get snow! Not just wet feathers, like New York.
What variety snow falls with and has: this kind lays like
    wet sheets
or soaked opaque blotting paper: where a surface makes
a natural puddle, its own melting darkens it, as though it
    had lain

all winter and the thaw is come. Is this change in weather in
    early April

just what the sugarbush needed, upstate and further up,
    New Hampshire, Vermont?

Maple syrup production is off, the *Times* says, due to the
    vogue for maple furniture.

Willingly or not, you can't give your Cape Cod cobbler's
    table

with a lamp attachment above a ship's-type wheel back to
    its grove.

Now it falls on two diagonals, except it's more: the depth
    dimension

of air. Ugh. The head of this household is going out in it.

Willingly or not, I'll check up on Central Park

where branches of sunshine were in bloom on Monday.

Sorting, wrapping, packing, stuffing

dirty socks in dirty sneakers
capless tubes of unguents among brushes and septic Band-
      Aids
adhesive flowers into spongy books
when the great bronze bell
sounds its great bronze bong
it will find a lifetime jar of Yuban Instant in my right hand,
in my left, Coleman's Mustard.
But how do you pack a blue fire escape – even if the man
got off it out of the 97 degree sun
and blizzards, then sullied snow that left
disclosing no car where one was. Excuse me, druggist,
can you take this blue fire escape out of my eye?
      (no, no one is going to ask anyone to take anything
      out of a heart, not even a tear with a hambone in it.
      All there is
      is blood and thump).

Now the blue fire escape
is packed, and it is
already tomorrow O little brown bat guano
of course it is still today
with the bay crinkling at the edges
of a tomorrow when Creeping Charlie and Stinking Willie
      flourish under glass on the moon.
Imagine going to the sun for the winter
if it's like Miami
Or getting an earth burn
Or

better we should slip into this Ice Age remnant granite
      boulder

and grab a snooze
it is too much like packing
on Saturn
where they have poison ivy like we have Himalayas
poisonous only to planets

                    give us a gingham smile
red white and checkered
Help
      the blue fire escape!
it's coming unpacked all over the floor like a Milky Way
lighting the north
an aurora borealis of neckties
                    Knize
                    Sulka
                    Au Chardon d'Ecosse
stuff wrap cram snap
      'Hello Lincoln?
      I want to store
      a blue fire escape.'

How pretty, rising from the long Memorial Pool
among toy boats all day and stars all night
glittering and cold as Santa Claus
                    'See you at The Petunia Pump.
                    More later.'

The time is getting out of hand
          splash splash
cut down the books
to fit an Oshkosh nutshell
          My Heart Is Like a Green Canoe
          The World Is a Long Engagement Party
          The Great Divorce Has Been Annulled

Romance of Serge Eisenstein
Immanuel Kant, Boy Detective
Emma Kant, Mother of Men
Judy Kant, R.N.
The spruce have stopped shrinking
they never began and great hunks of the world will fit

Crocus Night

The fire had struggled from my hand – *Susan Coolidge*

The heavy umbrellas
aren't worth their weight.
Doors swing and slam
checked by gusts. A whisperer
has a friendly reek.
A hell broth!
and hollows among clouds.
Then the moon goes crocus.

Milk

Milk used to come in tall glass, heavy and crystalline as frozen melted snow. It rose direct and thick as horse-chestnut tree trunks that do not spread out upon the ground even a little: a shaft of white drink narrowing at the cream and rounded off in a thick-lipped grin. Empty and unrinsed, a diluted milk ghost entrapped and dulled light and vision.

Then things got a little worse: squared, high-shouldered and rounded off in the wrong places, a milk replica of a handmade Danish wooden milk bat. But that was only the beginning. Things got worse than that.

Milk came in waxed paper that swelled and spilled and oozed flat pieces of milk. It had a little lid that didn't close properly or resisted when pulled so that when it did give way milk jumped out.

Things are getting better now. Milk is bigger – half-a-gallon, at least – in thin milky plastic with a handle, a jug founded on an oblong. Pick it up and the milk moves, rising enthusiastically in the neck as it shifts its center of weight. Heavy as a breast, but lighter, shaping itself without much changing shape: like bringing home the milk in a bandana, a neckerchief or a scarf, strong as canvas water wings whose strength was only felt dragged under water.

On the highway this morning at the go-round, about where you leave New Hampshire, there had been an accident. Milk was sloshed on the gray-blue-black so much like a sheet of early winter ice you drove over it slowly, no matter what the temperature of the weather that eddied in through the shatterproof glass gills. There were milk-skins all around, the way dessert plates look after everyone has left the table in the Concord grape season. Only bigger, unpigmented though pretty opaque, not squashed but no less empty.

Trembling, milk is coming into its own.

Poem

How about an oak leaf
if you had to be a leaf?
Suppose you had your life to live over
knowing what you know?
Suppose you had plenty money

'Get away from me you little fool.'

Evening of a day in early March,
you are like the smell of drains
in a restaurant where paté maison
is a slab of cold meat loaf
damp and wooly. You lack charm.

3/23/66

It's funny early spring weather, mild and washy
the color of a head cold.
The air rushes. Branches
are going nowhere, like the ocean,
spring salt unstopping sinuses. Winter salt doesn't.
Everything just sitting around: a barn without eaves,
a dumpy cottage set catty-corner
on its lot, a field with a horse in it.
A plane goes over, leaving its wake,
an awakening snore. A truck
passes, perceived as a quick shuffle
of solitaire cards. And the poor old humpy lawn
is tufted with Irish eyebrows of onion grass.
A chill on the nape smells frowsty
the spring no more awake
than a first morning stretch
and no more asleep. Growing
and going, in sight and sound, as the fire last night
looked out at us reading *Great Expectations* aloud
and fled up the chimney.

Now and Then

for Kenward Elmslie

Up from the valley
now and then a chain saw rising to a shriek, subsiding to a
    buzz
'Someone' is 'cutting in his wood lot' another day
shows they are not
someone is two men clearing shoulders
of a narrow high-crowned road
stacked poles were lately saplings
the leaves on the slash gone limp, unstarched, unsized
one man with one fierce eye and where the other should be
an ill-knit cicatrix
men who don't make much aren't much
for spending what they do
on glass eyes, tooth-straightening devices ('a mouth
like the back of a switchboard'), nose jobs, dewenning
    operations
a country look prevails
and a vestigial fear of the evil eye lurks
'... my skin creeps ...'
                       Out of Adamant Co-op
men in 'overhauls' step into evening rising
in long-shadowed bluish haze to gold and pink
by Sodom Lake (was it that any Bible name
was an OK name?) and boys stare unabashed
and unaggressive not what the man on the bus fled
from his one day job talking excitedly about
'teen-age Puerto Rican tail-bait' and
'You can *have* New York!' Some present
you'd rather have wouldn't you an apple tree
that climbed up into keels over

sad, and too bad, the best apples on Apple Hill
still, it can be propped or budded on new stock or just
that it once was there
                              Driving past, driving down, driving
                                    over
along the Winooski
through the home of Granite City Real Ice Cream
The Monument Capitol
buildings of rusticated granite marred
to our eyes by etched polished granite remodeled down-
    stairs
may be found by a future happily heterodox
'There's a touch of autumn –
                                    there's another touch of
                                        autumn'
and the dark tranquility of hemlocks encroaching on un-
    tilled fields
'You can't make a living
plowing stones' subsistence
farming is well out of style: 'You can't call it living
without the margin'
coveted obsolescence!
a margin like that on this page
a paper luxury 'Collectors'
the lady in the antique shop said 'Are snapping up
silver' 'Since we're off the silver standard?' 'Why,
maybe so' Perhaps
six 1827 Salem coin-silver spoons for $18
or what about
'Have you *The Pearl of Orr's Island*?'
'*That's* a book I'd want to read myself.
I'm from here but live in Florida.
Winters are too hard: 40 below.
You don't feel it though

like zero in Boston. I'll take St Johnsbury any day
over Boston.'
                    Over St Johnsbury the clouds shift in curds
and a street goes steeply down
into Frenchtown by the railroad station
into which anachronistically comes
a real train: yesterday's torment of dust-exhaling plush
on the backs of bare knees today's nostalgia
but not much. Curls cut out of wood, brick
of a certain cut and color, a hopped-up cripple
on a hill above his pond, a slattern
frowning at the early-closed state liquor store,
an attic window like a wink,
The Scale Co., St Johnsbury has everything
            Not this high hill a road
going in undergrowth leads up to
by walls of flat cleared-field stones
so many and so long a time to take
so much labor so long ago and so soon
to be going back, a host to hardhack
and blueberry baby steps
first fallings from a sky
in which the wind is moving furniture
the upholstery of summer coming all unstitched
the air full of flying kapok
and resolutions: 'remember to fetch the ax
whack back pine intrusions'
from the road turning down to a lower field
and across the roughest one the County keeps
a woman and a boy come up
on heavy horses. 'Morning!
Had frost
last night at Adamant.
Might have a killing frost

tonight.' Quick and clear as the water
where cress grows the cold
breaks on the hills to the soft crash
of a waterfall beyond
a beaver pond
and slides on
flinging imaginary fragments of cat's ice
from its edges to flash
a bright reality in the night sky and it –
the cold – stands, a rising pool, about
Sloven's farmhouse and he dreams
of dynamite. A bog sucks
at his foundations. Somewhere a deer
breaks branches. The trees
say *Wesson. Mazola*
replies a frog.

        It doesn't happen though the cold
that is not that night. It happens all right
not then when the white baneberry
leans secretively where a road forks
met with surprise: 'Why here it is:
the most beautiful thing.' The spirit
of Gelett Burgess sets Mother Nature
gabbing. '*That's* my Actea pachypoda, dear, we
call it Doll's-Eyes.' Got up as smart
as ever in muck and dank she belches
– ' 'Scuse: just a touch of gas' –
swamp maple flames and ambles over and plunks
down on a dead rubber tire
to contemplate smashed glass and a rusty tin
and 'some of my choicer bits: that
I call Doctor's Dentures. These
are Little Smellies.' Not
the sort you look to meet so near

gold-domed, out of scale Montpelier
a large-windowed kind of empty public bigness
so little to show, so much
to take pride in rather more than on the way to Stowe
a pyrocrafted maple board in a Gyp-o-teria
IF MORE MEN WERE SELF STARTERS
FEWER WIVES WOULD HAVE TO CRANK.
Welcome to the chair lift and cement chalet.

                        Days
of unambiguous morning when dawn
peels back like a petal to disclose blue depths
deep beyond all comprehending and tall field growth bends
with a crushing weight of water cut
into sac-shaped portions, each less than a carat
and which streak an early walker's trouser legs
'You're soaked!' crossing on a door
the spill to where nodding Ladies' Tresses
pallidly braid their fragrance and the woods
emit their hum. Days
when the pond holds on its steel one cloud
in which thin drowned trees stand
spare shapes of winter when summer
is just loosening to fall and bits of ribbon
from an electric typewriter patch a screen.
Croquet days, scissors-and-paste nights
after dinner on the better sort of ham
and coffee strong enough to float a goose egg.
Are those geese, that V, flying so early?
Can it be so late? in the green state
needles, leaves, fronds, blades, lichens and moss create
                    Can it be so soon before the long white
refrozen in frost on frost
on all twigs again will flash
cross cutting star streaks – the atoms

dance – on a treacherous night
in headlights?

                  'Horrible Cold Night
Remain at Home'

                  'Clear and Beautiful
Remain at Home'

MORE ABOUT PENGUINS
AND PELICANS

Penguinews, which appears every month, contains details of all the new books issued by Penguins as they are published. From time to time it is supplemented by *Penguins in Print*, which is a complete list of all available books published by Penguins. (There are well over four thousand of these.)

A specimen copy of *Penguinews* will be sent to you free on request. For a year's issues (including the complete lists) please send 30p if you live in the United Kingdom, or 60p if you live elsewhere. Just write to Dept EP, Penguin Books Ltd, Harmondsworth, Middlesex, enclosing a cheque or postal order, and your name will be added to the mailing list.

Note: *Penguinews* and *Penguins in Print* are not available in the U.S.A. or Canada

PENGUIN MODERN EUROPEAN POETS

This series now includes selected work by the following poets, in verse translations by, among others, W. H. Auden, Lawrence Ferlinghetti, Michael Hamburger, Ted Hughes, J. B. Leishman, Christopher Middleton and David Wevill:

Amichai	*Kovner/Sachs*
Apollinaire	*Montale*
Bobrowski/Bienek	*Pavese*
Celan	*Pessoa*
Ekelöf	*Popa*
Enzensberger	*Quasimodo*
Four Greek Poets:	*Rilke*
Cavafy/Elytis/Gatsos/Seferis	*Three Czech Poets:*
Grass	*Nezval/Bartušek/Hanzlík*
Guillevic	*Tsvetayeva*
Haavikko/Tranströmer	*Ungaretti*
Holan	*Weöres/Juhász*
Holub	*Yevtushenko*

SOME PENGUIN ANTHOLOGIES

POETRY OF THE FORTIES*
Edited by Robin Skelton

MODERN POETRY FROM AFRICA
Edited by Gerald Moore and Ulli Beier

THE PENGUIN BOOK OF RESTORATION VERSE
Edited by Harold Love

TWENTIETH-CENTURY GERMAN VERSE
Patrick Bridgwater

THE PENGUIN BOOK OF ENGLISH ROMANTIC
VERSE
Edited by David Wright

THE PENGUIN BOOK OF SATIRICAL VERSE
Edited by Edward Lucie-Smith

THE PENGUIN BOOK OF WELSH VERSE
Edited by Anthony Conran

THE PENGUIN BOOK OF ANIMAL VERSE
Edited by George MacBeth

THE PENGUIN BOOK OF ELIZABETHAN VERSE
Edited by Edward Lucie-Smith

THE MID-CENTURY ENGLISH POETRY 1940–60*
Edited by David Wright

THE PENGUIN BOOK OF JAPANESE VERSE
Edited by Geoffrey Bownas and Anthony Thwaite

POETRY OF THE THIRTIES*
Edited by Robin Skelton

POETRY OF THE NINETIES
Edited by R. K. R. Thornton

*NOT FOR SALE IN THE U.S.A.

WILLIAM WORDSWORTH: THE PRELUDE
A PARALLEL TEXT

EDITED BY J. C. MAXWELL

Wordsworth's great autobiographical poem, subtitled *Growth of a Poet's Mind*, was completed in 1805–6. During the rest of his life his interest in the work persisted, and the poem was several times revised, to be published soon after his death in 1850. Originally intended as the first part of a massive three-part poem, *The Prelude* contains some of the greatest poetry Wordsworth wrote on those events and feelings of his youth which lie behind so much of his most powerful work.

Critics and readers have differed over the relative merits of the 1805–6 and 1850 versions of the poem. The two versions are here presented in parallel for the first time in a paperback edition, and the edition has been so designed as to enable the reader to follow either version without interruption, or to compare the versions should he so wish. The manuscripts have been re-examined and many errors in both texts corrected from manuscript evidence. The editor's introduction and notes comment on the manuscript history of the poem and deal with points of difficulty.

Also available

Robert Browing: The Ring and the Book
Edited by Richard D. Altick

Lord Byron: Don Juan
Edited by T. G. Steffan, W. W. Pratt and E. Steffan

John Donne: The Complete English Poems
Edited by A. J. Smith

Samuel Johnson: The Complete English Poems
Edited by J. D. Fleeman

Christopher Marlowe: The Complete Poems and Translations
Edited by Stephen Orgel

Sir Gawain and the Green Knight
Edited by J. A. Burrow

PENGUIN EDUCATION BOOKS

POET TO POET

In the introductions to their personal selections from the work of poets they have admired, the individual editors write as follows:

Crabbe Selected by C. Day Lewis

'As his poetry displays a balance and decorum in its versification, so his moral ideal is a kind of normality to which every civilized being should aspire. This, when one looks at the desperate expedients and experiments of poets (and others) today, is at least refreshing.'

Henryson Selected by Hugh MacDiarmid

'There is now a consensus of judgement that regards Henryson as the greatest of our great makars. Literary historians and other commentators in the bad period of the century preceding the twenties of our own century were wont to group together as the great five: Henryson, Dunbar, Douglas, Lyndsay, and King James I; but in the critical atmosphere prevailing today it is clear that Henryson (who was, with the exception of King James, the youngest of them) is the greatest.'

Herbert Selected by W. H. Auden

'The two English poets, neither of them, perhaps, major poets, whom I would most like to have known well, are William Barnes and George Herbert.

'Even if Isaac Walton had never written his life, I think that any reader of his poetry will conclude that George Herbert must have been an exceptionally good man, and exceptionally nice as well.'

POET TO POET

Whitman Selected by Robert Creeley

'If Whitman has taught me anything, and he has taught me a great deal, often against my own will, it is that the common *is* personal, intensely so, in that having no-one thus to invest it, the sea becomes a curious mixture of water and table salt and the sky the chemical formula for air. It is, paradoxically, the personal which makes the common in so far as recognizes the existence of the many in the one. In my own joy or despair, I am brought to that which others have also experienced.'

Tennyson Selected by Kingsley Amis

'England notoriously had its doubts as well as its certainties, its neuroses as well as its moral health, its fits of gloom and frustration and panic as well as its complacency. Tennyson is the voice of those doubts and their accompaniments, and his genius enabled him to communicate them in such a way that we can understand them and feel them as our own. In short we know from experience just what he means. Eliot called him the saddest of all English poets, and I cannot improve on that judgement.'

Also available:

Wordsworth *Selected by Lawrence Durrell*
Cotton *Selected by Geoffrey Grigson*
Jonson *Seected by Thom Gunn*
Shelley *Selected by Kathleen Raine*
Pope *Selected by Peter Levi*

PENGUIN MODERN POETS

1* Lawrence Durrell   Elizabeth Jennings   R. S. Thomas
2* Kingsley Amis   Dom Moraes   Peter Porter
3* George Barker   Martin Bell   Charles Causley
4* David Holbrook   Christopher Middleton   David Wevill
5† Gregory Corso   Lawrence Ferkinghetti   Allen Ginsberg
6 George MacBeth   Edward Lucie-Smith   Jack Clemo
7* Richard Murphy   Jon Silkin   Nathaniel Tarn
8* Edwin Brock   Geoffrey Hill   Stevie Smith
9† Denise Levertov   Kenneth Rexroth   William Carlos Williams
10 Adrian Henri   Roger McGrough   Brian Patten
11 D. M. Black   Peter Redgrove   D. M. Thomas
12* Alan Jackson   Jeff Nuttall   William Wantling
13 Charles Bukowski   Philip Lamantia   Harold Norse
14 Alan Brownjohn   Michael Hamburger   Charles Tomlinson
15 Alan Bold   Edward Brathwaite   Edwin Morgan
16 Jack Beeching   Harry Guest   Matthew Mead
17 W. S. Graham   Kathleen Raine   David Gascoyne
18 A. Alvarez   Roy Fuller   Anthony Thwaite
19 John Ashbery   Lee Harwood   Tom Raworth
20 John Heath-Stubbs   F. T. Prince   Stephen Spender
21* George Mackay Brown   Norman MacCaig   Iain Crichton Smith
22* John Fuller   Peter Levi   Adrian Mitchell
23 Geoffrey Grigson   Edwin Muir   Adrian Stokes